glass
A Short History

David Whitehouse

THE BRITISH MUSEUM PRESS

in association with
The Corning Museum of Glass, Corning, New York

First published in 2012 by
The British Museum Press
A division of the British Museum
Company Ltd
38 Russell Square
London WC1B 3QQ

britishmuseum.org/publishing

in association with
The Corning Museum of Glass
1 Museum Way
Corning NY 14830
United States

A catalogue record for this book is available
from the British Library

ISBN 978 0 7141 5086 4

Designed by James Alexander, Jade Design

Printed in China by
C&C Offset Printing Co. Ltd

Frontispiece Jug of colourless glass with
applied opaque white and blue stripes. Made
at Beykoz near Istanbul, Turkey. 19th century.
H. 25.6 cm. British Museum, 1877,1015.4,
given by Edmund Christy.

Author acknowledgements
Connoisseurs and curators have admired
and collected glass for centuries. Two of the
objects described in these pages have been
treasured for two hundred years or more.

This book is the most recent fruit of
our ongoing fascination with glass. It has
benefitted not only from the researches
of colleagues at the British Museum and
The Corning Museum of Glass but also of
individuals and institutions worldwide. In
particular, I am grateful to Emma Poulter,
Axelle Russo-Heath and Rosemary Bradley
at The British Museum Press. Thanks also to
those who provided images: the Department
of Photography and Imaging at the British
Museum and Mary Chervenak and the
Photographic Department at The Corning
Museum of Glass.

Contents

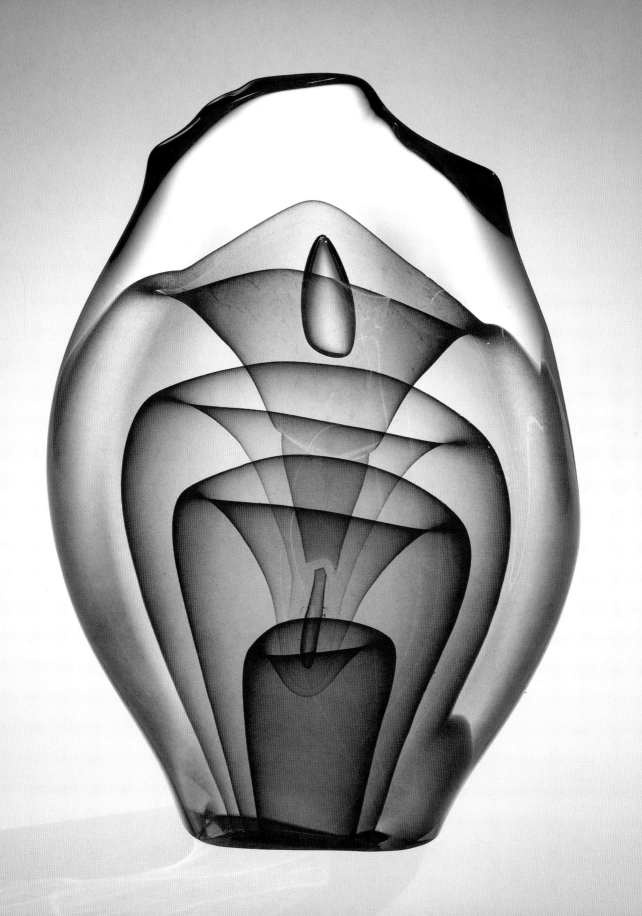

Preface

Since its discovery more than 4000 years ago, glass has served an extraordinary variety of purposes. Most of us cannot imagine our homes, or indeed our lives, without it. Glass has played an essential role in science – in telescopes and scientific apparatus – and artists throughout the ages have delighted in its properties and fragile beauty. The possibilities are endless.

I cannot remember how many times I have been asked the deceptively simple question: can you recommend a book about the history of glass? The answer, of course, is: yes. Excellent studies exist of one or another aspect of glass history and there are scholarly books about the entire history of glass; some of them are listed on pages 123–4. But it is difficult to identify a book that provides a short, readable overview. This book attempts to satisfy this demand.

Albeit short, and with the exception of two major categories, it contains a summary of the history of glass and glassmaking. The first exception is flat glass (that is, stained glass, window panes and mirrors) and the second is modern industrial production. Introductions to these subjects are suggested on page 124.

The book is illustrated with images of rare and beautiful glasses from the collections of the British Museum and The Corning Museum of Glass. At the British Museum, the glass is integrated with objects executed in other media, providing a unique opportunity to see the achievements of great glassmakers in the context of the world in which they worked. At Corning, the entire museum is devoted to the history of glass and glassmaking.

In the following pages you will find the history of glass told against the background of the cultures that discovered and manipulated the unique properties of this material from its ancient origins to the present day. I hope, of course, that you enjoy the book; but, much more important, I hope it encourages you to look at, and learn about, the art and history of glass.

David Whitehouse
The Corning Museum of Glass, Corning, New York

'Emergence Four-Stage', Dominick Labino (1910–87). Labino's sculptures are icons of the early Studio Glass Movement (see p. 103). The experimental colours of his 'Emergence' series were inspired by analyses of the chemical composition of the 4th-century AD Lycurgus Cup (see pp. 38–9). Hot-worked glass with airtraps, Ohio, United States, 1975. H. 22.4 cm. Corning Museum of Glass, 76.4.21, purchased with the aid of funds from the National Endowment for the Arts.

Introduction: glass and glassmaking

The virtuosity of Venetian glassmakers during the Renaissance is exemplified by these vessels made of colourless glass, known as *cristallo*. The smaller glass, made about 1600, has a stem in the form of an owl. The stem of the larger vessel, which dates from the late 16th century, represents Pulcinella (usually called Punchinello in English), a stock character in Italian *Commedia dell'Arte*, noted for his long nose and his mean and devious ways. Blown, mould-blown and applied glass, Venice, Italy, c.1600. H. (larger glass) 30.5 cm. British Museum, S.461, bequeathed by Felix Slade.

The Roman polymath, Pliny the Elder, in *Natural History*, an encyclopaedia completed by AD 78, told the story of how (it was thought) glass had been discovered. Sailors disembarked on the coast of modern Lebanon from a ship carrying a cargo of the mineral natron, in order to cook a meal. Failing to find stones suitable for supporting their cauldrons over the fire, they used instead chunks of natron from the ship. 'When these became heated and were completely mingled with the sand on the beach a strange liquid flowed in streams; and this, it is said, was the origin of glass.'

Pliny knew that sand is the largest constituent of glass and that the mineral natron is one of the alkaline substances used by early glassmakers to lower the melting point of the sand. But his story, however picturesque, is just that: a story. The true story of glass – how its manufacture and uses have changed over the centuries – is far more complex and engaging. It has been pieced together from the written evidence, archaeological discoveries and above all the examination of glass objects in museums, the cabinets of collectors and the scientists' laboratories. The story is incomplete, however. There are gaps waiting to be filled and the beginning of the story in particular is sketchy in the extreme – finds datable to the very first centuries of glassmaking are very rare indeed; they consist of beads and a few shapeless scraps. Nevertheless, the outlines are clear and, for some periods and places, we know a surprising amount of detail.

Glass exists in nature, most often in the form of obsidian, which is created during volcanic eruptions. People, however, have been making glass for more than 4000 years. After an introduction to the science and techniques behind glassmaking, this book chronicles the major developments in glass over the last 4000 years – from its early beginnings in ancient Mesopotamia and the Romans' discovery of glass-blowing which revolutionized the industry, to the fine cut and gilded glass produced by the Islamic world, the luxury glass of later Europeans, and the art and uses of modern glass. Highlighting the remarkable achievements of the craftsmen and artists who have worked with this extraordinary medium, *Glass: A Short History* reminds us why this unique material has figured so highly in daily life and art throughout the ages and why it remains a fundamental material for industry and artistic expression today.

What is glass, and how is it made?

Most glass consists of minerals that are heated until they melt, and are cooled at a rate that prevents them from resuming the crystalline structure of the original ingredients. Hot glass is liquid. As it cools, it becomes viscous until, when cold, it is rigid and has the properties of a solid but, because of the way it cooled, it retains the random structure of a liquid. Consequently, glass can be softened by reheating, and shaped and softened repeatedly until the object is completed.

The process of making glass can be divided into three parts: primary production, when the ingredients are melted to make raw glass; secondary production, when the raw glass is melted again to make objects, and sometimes decorated with molten glass before being carefully cooled (a process called annealing); and tertiary production, where the annealed object is decorated, for example by engraving. Tertiary production is most efficient when the artisan has a convenient source of freshly annealed objects, known as 'blanks', awaiting decoration.

Primary production

Traditionally, most glass contains three ingredients: silica (usually in the form of sand), soda or potash (which acts as a flux and lowers the temperature at which the sand melts) and lime (calcium oxide, which gives stability to an otherwise unstable combination). Sand is readily available in most places. Depending on the time and place, soda came either in the form of the mineral trona (natron) or as ash derived from plants growing in salty environments. In Europe, potash was made by burning beech leaves or ferns. Although an essential component, early glassmakers seem to have added the third ingredient, calcium, inadvertently, as an impurity either in the silica (sand collected on the seashore may contain shells) or in the soda (plants growing in soil derived from limestone may contain calcium). The addition of oxides gives the glass colour (cobalt, for example, makes it blue) or removes unwanted colours caused by impurities in the basic ingredients.

Melting the raw materials requires temperatures of 1000–1100°C (about 1800–2050°F). In pre-Roman times in Western Asia, where glassmaking began, and in the Mediterranean region, furnaces capable of reaching

A seated man formed by casting molten glass in a mould. Found in China, the figurine is of translucent green glass that imitates the colour of jade, the name given to two minerals (jadeite and nephrite), both of which were highly prized in China. Tang period (AD 618–906). H. 4.3 cm. British Museum, 1938,0524.599.

these temperatures were small and consequently in any one firing only a few small crucibles of glass were produced. The small scale of production, combined with the highly specialized knowledge required to select and mix the raw materials and to maintain and operate the furnaces, meant that glass objects were greatly prized. Indeed, they were often as highly prized as the precious and semi-precious gems they sometimes imitated.

With the discovery of glass-blowing in the early to mid-first century BC, glassmaking was transformed. By blowing into a mass of molten glass on the end of a tube, glassworkers realized they could inflate the glass just as one inflates a balloon. From here on glassworkers had the ability to make glassware quickly and inexpensively, and the demand for glass increased substantially. In order to meet the demands of the glassblowers and the marketplace, glassmakers needed to develop furnaces with a greater capacity for melting glass. In 1964, a single slab of glass weighing nine tonnes came to light at Beit She'arim in Israel. The slab turned out to be the unused contents of a revolutionary type of furnace. Known as a reverberatory furnace, it consisted of a rectangular tank with a low roof, a combustion chamber at one end and a vent at the other. The furnace was operated by partly filling the tank with raw materials. Workers stoked the fire continuously to provide heat, which was drawn through the tank by the draught created by the vent. As it did so, the heat radiated from the roof and melted the raw materials. Using such furnaces, glassmakers could melt several tonnes of raw materials at a time. In the early centuries AD, tank furnaces in present-day Lebanon, Israel and Egypt supplied raw glass to glassworkers all over the Roman Empire.

Secondary production
Before the discovery of glass-blowing, glassworkers shaped molten glass in several ways. Some of the earliest objects were pendants, beads and amulets made by pouring or pressing glass into open moulds, a technique learned from metalworkers.

This core-formed (see page 13) bottle is in the form of a bolti (*Tilapia nilotica*), a fish that abounds in the River Nile and has been eaten for millennia. The small mouth suggests that the bottle held a liquid substance, possibly scented oil. Made in Egypt, it was found at el-Amarna, the short-lived capital of Egypt built by Pharaoh Akhenaten about 1353 BC and abandoned shortly afterwards. 18th Dynasty (c.1352–1336 BC). L. 14.5 cm. British Museum, 1921,1008.127, donated by the Egypt Exploration Society.

A much more refined technique, also acquired from metalworkers, was the *cire perdue* or lost wax method of casting, in which the desired object was modelled in wax. The model was coated with fine clay, leaving just a few small holes. The clay-covered model was then heated, causing the clay to become earthenware and the wax to melt and escape through the holes. The earthenware was now a mould, the interior of which was exactly the size and shape of the wax model. When making the glass cast, the raw materials may have been introduced in powdered form and melted in the mould.

Most of the earliest glass vessels, all of which are small, were made by a technique unique to glassmaking known as core-forming. A core, probably made of animal dung mixed with clay, was attached to a metal rod and modelled to the size and shape of the interior of the vessel. The core was covered with glass, either by dipping it in a crucible of molten glass or by coating it with powdered glass in a liquid medium and heating the powder until it fused. Decoration was added by applying trails of molten glass and dragging them up and down to create featherlike patterns. At the end of the process, the core was removed from the interior of the vessel with a metal tool. Core-forming, invented in the sixteenth century BC, continued to be used until the discovery of glass-blowing 1500 years later.

In the early to mid-first century BC, with the discovery that glass could be blown (see p. 11), glassworkers learned they could control not only the size of the bubble but also its shape, by manipulating it with simple hand-held tools. Within three or four generations, glassworkers realized that an object can be formed and decorated in a single operation by inflating the bubble inside a decorated mould.

Tertiary production

After annealing (the process of carefully cooling the glass), glass objects can be decorated by painting, gilding, engraving, cutting or etching.

Painting on glass consists of either enamelling or cold-painting. Enamelling requires the painter to apply powdered glass of various colours suspended in an oily medium, which is fused by heating in a kiln or at the mouth of the furnace. Cold painting is the application of paint such as artists use on other materials. Reverse painting involves creating an image on the back of the glass, which is intended to be seen from the front. Because of this, the painter must apply the colours in the reverse of the normal order, beginning with highlights and ending with the background. Gilding is the application of gold either in the form of foil or leaf, or as powder in a liquid medium.

The simplest kind of engraving on glass is scratching the surface with a pointed tool. In recent centuries, glass engravers have used tools mounted with diamond chips, but other minerals with a hardness greater than 7 on the Mohs scale (for example, corundum) serve equally well. Stippling is the technique of using an engraving tool to tap on the surface of the glass. Each tap makes a tiny mark and the design is made up of hundreds or thousands of marks. Engraving can also be accomplished by holding a glass object against a rotating stone or copper wheel fed with an abrasive slurry. Glass cutting involves removing glass from the surface of an object by grinding it with rotating wheels. The last stage in the process involves polishing the ground surface to produce the brilliant, often glittering effect we associate with cut glass.

Decorators can also use hydrofluoric acid to etch the surface. Typically, acid-etched ornament is produced by covering an object with an acid-resistant substance, such as wax, through which the decoration is scratched. The object is then immersed in hydrofluoric acid, which attacks the exposed areas of the surface. Glass dipped in a mixture of hydrofluoric and sulphuric acids has a glossy, polished appearance.

Identifying early techniques: a note of caution
Very few descriptions of the techniques used by glassworkers before the Middle Ages have survived. Our understanding of how early glass objects were made, therefore, is based on close inspection of the objects themselves. Seams on the surface of a mould-blown vessel, for example, show that it was formed in a mould with more than one part. Information can also be gleaned from knowledge of how similar pieces are made today, and from experiments aimed to reproduce not only the form of an early object but also the unintended but revealing traces of its manufacturing process, such as the faint marks left by jacks on a rim. We must be aware, however, that experimental archaeology shows how an object can be made; it does not necessarily show how it was made. Consequently, controversy still surrounds the techniques used to make such objects as Roman cameo glasses (p. 32) and cage cups (pp. 37–9).

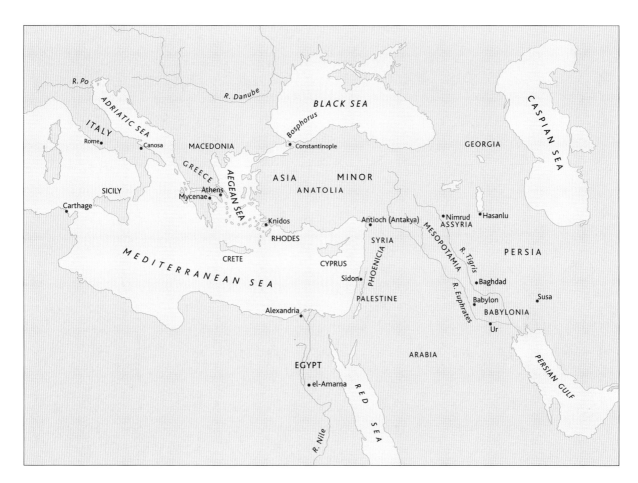

There are a number of historical sites referenced in this book. The above map of Europe, North Africa and the Near East shows the location of these sites – some of the principal glassmaking centres discussed in the first six chapters.

Glass before glass-blowing

Archaeologists believe that the first man-made glass was produced in Mesopotamia (present-day Iraq and northern Syria) during the Bronze Age, about 2300 BC. The first few centuries of glassmaking, however, are represented by just a handful of finds, mostly shapeless lumps, and so our knowledge of the origins of this new material is sketchy in the extreme.

Mesopotamia, Egypt and the Eastern Mediterranean, c.1550–1070 BC
We reach firmer ground in the mid-sixteenth century BC, when the first glass vessels were made, in northern Mesopotamia. These objects, all small, were made by the technique unique to glassmaking known as core-forming, in which glass is shaped around a removable core (see p. 13). Examples of glassware from this time show that Mesopotamian glassworkers experimented with the use of colour and pattern. They made mosaic glass vessels by fusing slices of canes (glass rods of various colours, sometimes with simple designs visible in cross section) arranged in patterns and attached to removable cores, and also made a variety of plaques and pendants formed in open moulds. The glass used to produce these early objects was brightly coloured by the addition of an oxide to the raw materials: for instance, cobalt oxide to make deep blue, antimony to make yellow, and so on.

We know more about early glassmaking in Egypt than in Mesopotamia, partly because of the ancient Egyptian custom of burying with the dead objects needed in the afterlife, and partly because of Egypt's dry climate, which is conducive to the preservation of glass. (Long-term exposure to moisture often causes glass to deteriorate, a process usually called 'weathering'.) The earliest closely datable glass objects from Egypt include beads and amulets, buried with the dead, each of which is engraved with the name of a pharaoh or his consort: Ahmose (r. 1550–1525 BC), his wife Ahmose-Nofretiti (d. about 1506 BC), Amenhotep I (r. 1525–1504 BC) and Queen Hatshepsut (r. 1479–1458 BC).

The first core-formed vessels were made in Mesopotamia in the 16th century BC. This typical Mesopotamian bottle, made of dark brown glass (now weathered to grey) and turquoise blue, was excavated from a 13th-century grave at the Sumerian city of Ur in southern Iraq. The ridges and grooves and the zigzag ornament were made by dragging a tool with a blunt end up and down the bottle while the glass was still soft. H. 11.8 cm. British Museum, 1928,1009.147.

Opposite One of the earliest closely datable glass vessels, this core-formed cosmetic jug bears a hieroglyphic inscription that includes a reference to Pharaoh Tuthmosis III, who reigned between about 1479 BC and 1425 BC, during the 18th Dynasty (1550–1295 BC). The blue glass imitates turquoise, while the yellow glass and enamel and the white glass probably imitate gold and silver. The inscription, stylized trees and other motifs are the earliest occurrence in Egypt of glass decorated with enamel. H. 9 cm. British Museum, 1868,1102.220.

The first core-formed vessels known to have been made in Egypt date from the reign of Tuthmosis III (c.1479–1425 BC), who campaigned in Syria and may have returned with glassmakers among his prisoners of war. These Egyptian vessels imitated the shapes of objects made in other materials, such as pottery and stone. They also simulated the colours of off-white alabaster and semi-precious stone, such as light blue turquoise and deep blue lapis lazuli (in Mesopotamia, Akkadian documents refer to '[genuine] lapis from the mountain' and '[imitation] lapis from the kiln'), indicating that early glassmakers were quick to discover and exploit the jewel-like properties of glass and its decorative possibilities. One of the earliest closely datable Egyptian vessels is a turquoise-blue jug decorated with white, yellow and deep blue spots and trails, and yellowish enamel. Bearing the throne-name of Tuthmosis III, it is therefore no later than 1425 BC. Other glass objects included mosaic glass vessels, personal ornaments including beads, amulets, earrings and pendants, and inlays and miniature sculptures. Throughout this period, glassmaking was a highly specialized skill, perhaps confined to royal workshops, and glass objects were highly sought-after, mostly as containers of costly cosmetics and perhaps medicinal preparations, and items of personal adornment. Glassmaking continued in Egypt until the end of the New Kingdom (about 1070 BC), after which, at a time of widespread collapse of states and cities, glass seems to have gone out of use. With the collapse of the most advanced technologies in lands

Right This plaque depicts a naked female, usually identified as Astarte, the Phoenician goddess of fertility. Made between 1400 BC and 1200 BC, it was found at Alalakh, an archaeological site in northern Syria. After centuries of burial, the deep blue glass has deteriorated and the surface is now dull bluish grey. H. 8.5 cm. British Museum, 1939,0613.76.

Right Amenhotep II ruled Egypt from about 1426 BC to 1400 BC. He is the probable subject of this miniature sculpture, one of the earliest known portraits in glass. Cast in bright blue glass by the lost wax process, the sculpture is now pale brown due to weathering. Egypt, c.1426–1400 BC. H. 4 cm. Corning Museum of Glass, 79.1.4.

Opposite Most ancient Egyptian core-formed glass is readily distinguishable from vessels made in Mesopotamia because the shapes are different. Finds from datable tombs, for example, show that jars of this type were popular in Egypt during the reigns of Pharaohs Amenhotep III and Akhenaten (c.1390–1336 BC). The wide mouth suggests that the jar contained a viscous ointment. H. 8.7 cm. British Museum, EA 4741.

bordering the Mediterranean, systems of production and distribution were shattered, and all luxury items, including glass, were severely affected.

While glassmaking flourished in Egypt and Western Asia, distinctive core-formed vessels were also made in Cyprus, and the Mycenaeans in Greece cast equally distinctive beads and pendants (from about the fourteenth to the twelfth century BC) usually by re-melting imported glass. Indeed, apparently from the beginning of glassmaking, the melting of raw materials to make raw glass ingots and the re-melting of ingots to make

objects were separate activities performed by different people, sometimes in different places. Glassmaking declined in these regions at about the same time as it declined in Egypt, because of the very reasons mentioned on p. 20.

Western Asia and the Mediterranean, c.900–300 BC
In the ninth century BC, powerful states, urban life and markets revived, and so did the manufacture and use of glass. Glass first reappeared as inlays in ivory plaques and panels that adorned fine furniture made by the Phoenicians, who inhabited the region of modern Lebanon. This luxurious furniture was exported to Iran, where fragments were found in ninth-century BC deposits at Hasanlu, and to Syria and Iraq, where the largest number of finds was made at Nimrud. However, pendants and beads in the form of human and animal heads are by far the most widely known type of Phoenician glass. These amulets, in use in the seventh to third centuries BC, were probably intended to bring the wearer luck and protection from danger.

Among the other finds from Nimrud are transparent greenish bowls apparently made by placing a disc over a hemispherical mould and reheating it until the glass softened and assumed the shape of the mould. A jar from the same site (p. 22) has an engraved cuneiform inscription giving the name of Sargon II (r. 722–705 BC), king of Assyria, indicating once again that fine glass objects were held in great esteem.

Left The 'Sargon Vase' was found in 1845–7 during excavations in the Northwest Palace at Nimrud, the capital of the Assyrian Empire from the 13th century BC to 706 BC, when King Sargon II moved to Khorsabad, thus making it the new capital. The object was cast and presumably ground and polished (although weathering has removed the original surface). The vase bears a scarcely visible inscription naming Sargon (r. 722–705 BC) and this allows us to date it to the late 8th century BC. H. 8.8 cm. British Museum, N.2070.

Right This pendant in the form of a bearded male head was formed around a removable metal rod or mandrel. Each curl of the hair and beard was made and applied separately. The eyes and eyebrows were also applied. Pendants and beads shaped like animal and human heads were popular in the eastern Mediterranean, home of the Phoenicians, and they were made in large numbers at Carthage, the Phoenician colony in Tunisia. Mid-4th to 3rd century BC. H. 6.2 cm. British Museum, 1906,0627.33.

With the revival of glassmaking, core-formed vessels reappeared; the earliest examples were buried in the late eighth century BC. Although the shapes are unlike earlier core-formed vessels, the manufacturing technique was the same, perhaps indicating that glassmaking was not completely abandoned in the eleventh century BC. Knowledge of core-forming spread to the eastern Mediterranean and between the mid-sixth century BC and the beginning of the first century AD, the largest numbers of glass vessels made in the Mediterranean region were small core-formed bottles and jars intended to contain scented oil and other cosmetics. By this time, these objects were produced in such quantity that it is clear that, in this part of the world, glassware, although still highly regarded, had ceased to be an exclusively luxury item.

By the fifth century BC, the Achaemenid Empire had expanded from its homeland in Iran to include Egypt and western and central Asia. The finest Achaemenid glass consists of luxurious cast, cut and polished tableware, the forms of which imitate vessels of precious metal. Much of this glass is almost colourless, like rock crystal, and the cold-working is superb. The oldest datable example of Achaemenid cast and cut glass was found at Aslaia in Libya, in a tomb that also contained fine pottery from Attica in

Below This exquisite cast and cut bowl was made in the Achaemenid Empire between about 500 BC and 400 BC. The form copies gold and silver *phialai* (Greek: bowls for drinking or pouring libations) and the almost colourless glass imitates rock crystal. A similar fragmentary example from Persepolis must be earlier than 331 BC, when this palace complex was destroyed by Alexander the Great. Diam. 17.5 cm. Corning Museum of Glass, 59.1.578.

Right Small core-formed containers, mostly for cosmetic preparations, remained in use in the Mediterranean until they were superseded by blown vessels at the beginning of the 1st century AD. This unusually large core-formed jar, shaped like an earthenware amphora, is a late example, made in the eastern Mediterranean in the 2nd or 1st century BC. H. 24 cm. Corning Museum of Glass, 55.1.62.

Above Core-forming revived in northern Mesopotamia at about the same time as cast and cut vessels came into use (see the 'Sargon Vase', p. 22). One of the new shapes was a cylindrical bottle with two small handles. Similar bottles have been found in the eastern Mediterranean (this example was found in Rhodes, Greece) and it is thought that they inspired local glassmakers to experiment with core-forming. Indeed, this object may have been made locally. *c.*700–600 BC. H. 16 cm. British Museum, 1860,0404.97.

Left The Athenian playwright Menander (d. about 292 BC) wrote comedies of manners that remained popular long after his death. The same stock characters appeared in more than one play and the actors wore distinctive masks to make the characters instantly recognizable. This tiny plaque, made from two slices of the same mosaic glass cane, shows the mask which represented a brothel keeper. Late 1st century BC to mid-1st century AD. H. 2.8 cm. Corning Museum of Glass, 66.1.78.

Below These colourless vessels were found, with seven others, in a tomb at Canosa in southern Italy. All three were cast, ground and polished. The bowl in the centre is decorated with gold foil sandwiched between two almost identical glass vessels, which were reheated until they fused. The objects were perhaps made in Alexandria, c.275–200 BC. H. (of centre bowl) 12 cm. British Museum, 1871,0518.2, donated by Felix Slade.

Greece, made about 430–425 BC. It is thought that production of this sort continued for about a century, and was restricted to objects for the use of the rich and powerful.

The Hellenistic and early Roman periods, 323 BC–c. AD 50
Between 334 and 326 BC, Alexander the Great conquered much of the eastern Mediterranean and western and central Asia. After Alexander died in 323 BC, his empire was divided into several kingdoms. One of these, ruled by the Ptolemaic dynasty, had as its capital Alexandria in Egypt. It survived as an independent state until the Romans conquered Egypt in 31 BC. Here, as elsewhere in the Mediterranean region and parts of Asia, the period between 323 and 31 BC is known as the Hellenistic period.

Ruled by a dynasty of Macedonian descent and with a majority of Egyptian inhabitants, Hellenistic Alexandria became one of the largest and richest cities in the Mediterranean. Its products, including fine glassware, reflect the wealth, artistry and cosmopolitan nature of the population.

The manufacture of mosaic glass, which had ceased in Egypt in the thirteenth century BC, was revived during the reign of Pharaoh Nectanebo II (c.360–343 BC) and was taken to a new level of complexity in the Hellenistic period. The production of mosaic glass plaques and inlays with intricate designs was accomplished in several stages. First, glass rods of different colours were assembled in a bundle with the desired pattern visible at the ends. The bundle was heated until the rods softened and, upon cooling, fused to form a single cane. Several such canes could be bundled, heated and fused to make complex, often pictorial designs. At any stage in the assembly of the design, the bundle of canes could be heated and stretched. As the cane became longer, the cross section became smaller but, however

small the design, every detail was preserved. The last stage in the process was cutting the cane into thin slices, all of which had identical ornament.

Most of these cane slices were made into inlays to decorate furniture, shrines and other objects. Their ornament centred around Egyptian beliefs and included traditional motifs, such as images of gods and sacred animals, and Greek elements, such as acanthus leaves and honeysuckle flowers. A surviving group of square and rectangular plaques, however, are decorated unusually with masks worn by characters in Greek theatrical productions (p. 26). It has been suggested that they were the equivalent of theatre tickets, although some are known to have been used as inlays.

Hellenistic glassworkers in Alexandria and other Mediterranean cities also produced the first ever services of glassware for eating and drinking. These spectacular objects were formed by various methods of fusing and slumping, and finished by cutting and polishing. The vessels include monochrome cups, bowls, kraters (bowls for mixing wine and water) and a large, two-handled jar. The monochrome objects are accompanied by mosaic glass plates, bowls and by gold 'sandwich' glasses, which are decorated with gold foil sandwiched between two fused layers of glass. These luxury objects, the use of which was confined to the wealthiest section of society, came into use in the mid- to late third century BC.

Monochrome, polychrome and mosaic glass vessels continued to be made in the first century of Roman rule. New forms appeared; one of the most common was a shallow bowl with vertical ribs made by slumping and manipulating a heated glass disc. More luxurious vessels were made from fused strips of half a dozen or more different colours of glass, sometimes with pieces of gold foil. The fused strips, which were narrow and seldom more than a few millimetres thick, consisted of either gold foil between two colourless layers or, more frequently, two layers of transparent coloured glass separated by an opaque white layer.

Left Slices of mosaic glass canes were fused and slumped to produce the two parts of this luxurious perfume bottle, which were ground and polished until they fitted perfectly. Pairs of perforations in the upper neck and at the shoulder indicate that the vessel originally had two opposed handles. Eastern Mediterranean, 3rd to 2nd century BC. H. 18.5 cm. Corning Museum of Glass, 58.1.38.

Right Mosaic glass made of lengths (not slices) of canes came into use in the 1st century BC and remained popular, especially in Italy, until the mid-1st century AD. In this example of 'ribbon' mosaic, each monochrome strip has a layer of opaque white glass sandwiched between transparent coloured strips. Italy, late 1st century BC to early 1st century AD. Diam. 8.6 cm. Corning Museum of Glass, 72.1.11.

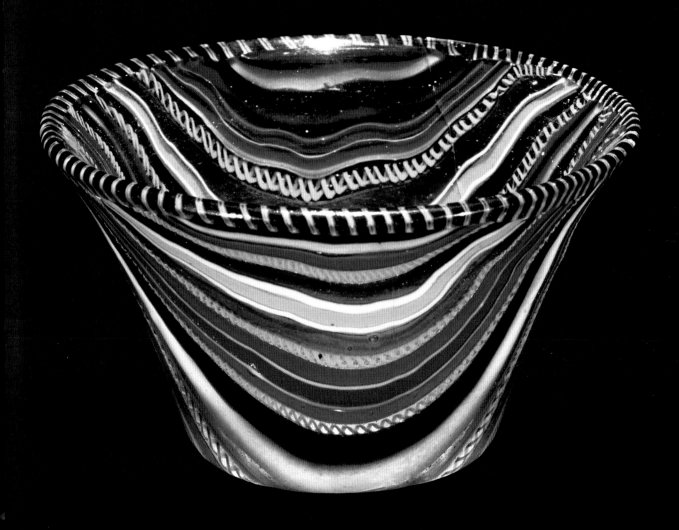

The glass of ancient Rome

For nearly 500 years, from the first century BC to the fifth century AD, the Romans ruled one of the largest empires that had ever existed. At its greatest extent, the Roman Empire reached from the Atlantic Ocean to the Persian Gulf and from the River Rhine to the Sahara Desert. It had an estimated population of about fifty million and in its heyday the capital, Rome, supported more than a million inhabitants. Like all ancient civilizations, its economy was based on agriculture and the overwhelming majority of the population worked on the land. Nevertheless, long-distance trade flourished and cargoes as diverse as marble and olive oil were shipped from one end of the Mediterranean to the other, and across country by road and river.

The Romans used more glass than any other civilization before the Renaissance. They discovered glass-blowing, the most significant breakthrough in the manufacture of glass since the invention of core-forming over 1500 years earlier. As a result, large quantities of inexpensive glassware became available throughout the Roman Empire. The Romans made the world's first window panes and decorated the interiors of buildings with glass panels and mosaics. Beads and other glass jewellery were common but at the same time, glassworkers produced exquisite luxury items, such as early Roman cameo glasses (p. 32) and late Roman cage cups (pp. 37–9)

Glass-blowing: a Roman discovery
In the early to mid-first century BC, glassmaking was transformed by the discovery that glass could be blown (see also p. 11). This discovery took place on or near the east coast of the Mediterranean, in present-day Lebanon or Israel. Finds from Jerusalem's Old City indicate that glassworkers were experimenting with the technique of inflating glass in the early decades of the first century BC. By the end of that century, glassmakers in the eastern Mediterranean were augmenting their production of core-formed or fused and slumped vessels with objects formed by blowing, and shortly afterwards glass-blowing became widespread. This new technique allowed glassmakers to make objects much more quickly, and in a much greater variety of sizes

and shapes, than was possible by earlier techniques. Consequently, in addition to producing relatively few luxury vessels, glassmakers now supplied vast numbers of inexpensive objects for daily use.

The discovery of glass-blowing was followed, in the first century AD, by the realization that glass can be formed and decorated in the same operation by inflating the bubble of molten glass in a decorated mould. Soon after this discovery, mould-blown vessels became available throughout the Roman Empire and beyond. Many first-century examples, blown in moulds with two or more parts, are often described as 'Sidonian', after the coastal city of Sidon (modern Saïda) in Lebanon, which Pliny the Elder, writing in AD 77, described as formerly an important centre of glassmaking. The ornament of early mould-blown objects sometimes includes inscriptions of the names of glassblowers or mould-makers. Among the latest Roman mould-made products are vessels with Christian or Jewish symbols, probably made in Jerusalem, and at other places in the Holy Land, in the sixth and seventh centuries.

Cameo glass

The rarest and most elaborate luxury glasses of the early Roman Empire are cameos. Inspired by engraved and relief-cut gems of banded semi-precious stones, such as agate and onyx, glassworkers covered plaques and vessels of one colour with one or more glass overlays of a different colour or colours, the preferred combination being opaque white over translucent deep blue. These undecorated 'blanks' were handed to a lapidary, who carved, ground and polished the ornament. It is generally agreed that cameo glasses were made during the reigns of Augustus, the first Roman emperor (r. 27 BC–AD 14), and his immediate successors, although a recent study of the unique collection in the British Museum led to the conclusion that, more precisely, they were created between about 15 BC and AD 25. A relatively large number of cameo fragments, including blanks, have been found in Rome – most likely the place of manufacture – in workshops that provided leading families with expensive luxuries.

Glass with applied decoration

In addition to using moulds, first-century AD glassblowers began to develop a large repertoire of decorating techniques. They rolled the partly formed objects in chips of coloured glass (perhaps in imitation of mosaic glass) or applied a small quantity of molten glass and drew it over the surface to make a pattern. The earliest Roman applied decoration, made in the first half of the first century, consists of thin trails wound spirally round the vessel. Later glassblowers were more adventurous and added zigzags and overall patterns of stripes and loops,

sometimes rolling the decoration on a flat surface until it was flush with the vessel's wall. Some of the most elaborate applied decoration made by the Romans consists of zoomorphic or, more often, plantlike or abstract motifs composed of sinuous, snakelike trails. These 'snake-thread' glasses were made in both the eastern and the north-western provinces of the empire, from the mid-second century until the early fourth century.

Cut and engraved glass
Glass with cut, engraved or wheel-abraded decoration was made for most of the first four centuries AD. We know very little about the tools used for these processes, although the information about the working of semi-

Far left Beaker with 'snake-thread' decoration. The decoration was produced by reheating the beaker and attaching to the surface small quantities of molten glass, which were drawn out and tooled to form dolphins and water plants. The beaker was made in the Rhineland in the 3rd or early 4th century. It was discovered at Worms, Germany. H. 20.4 cm. Corning Museum of Glass, 82.1.1

Left The mottled effect on this jar was obtained by reheating the partly formed vessel while it was still on the blowpipe, rolling it in loose fragments of coloured glass, reheating it again, and rolling it on a smooth surface until the fragments were flush. Acquired in Lebanon; made in the Mediterranean region, perhaps Italy, probably c. AD 50–75. H. 11.7 cm. Corning Museum of Glass, 59.1.88.

Right Colourless glass with overall patterns of wheel-cut facets were fashionable in the second half of the 1st century AD and the early 2nd century. Little is known about the techniques of cold-working glass, although they were probably the same as those described by Pliny the Elder for engraving semi-precious stones. Italy, AD 7–120. H. 12 cm. British Museum, 1856,1226.1203, bequeathed by Sir William Temple.

precious stones, recorded by Pliny the Elder (died AD 79) and others, probably also applies at least in part to the cold-working of glass; indeed, the same craftsmen may have worked with both materials.

The simplest cut or engraved decoration consisted of groups of incised horizontal lines on drinking vessels and bottles. Such objects were common at Pompeii and Herculaneum in Italy, when the cities were destroyed by the eruption of Vesuvius in AD 79. By this time, objects with overall patterns of hollow facets, reminiscent of honeycombs, were also fashionable all over the Roman Empire. They continued in use well into the second century.

A new variety of cut glass appeared towards the middle of the second century. The objects are decorated with scenes containing figures that include characters from mythology identified by Greek inscriptions. The figures are represented with facet-cut outlines, limbs and other major features, and scratched details. The earliest datable example consists of fragments of a bowl depicting the mythological story of Artemis and Actaeon, found at Dura-Europos in Syria and so presumably earlier than the destruction of the site in AD 256. (Actaeon was a hunter, who happened upon the goddess Diana bathing in a pool. As punishment, Diana turned Actaeon into a stag and he was torn to pieces by his hounds.)

In the fourth century, several styles of pictorial decoration were produced in different parts of the empire. These regional styles exemplified how vast and culturally diverse the empire was. Frequent finds from Rome and the nearby port of Ostia suggest that distinctive dishes and bowls, with figures defined by carefully incised outlines and with bodies and limbs represented

Left The 'Populonia Bottle' takes its name from the ancient city of Populonia (near modern Piombino, Italy), where it was discovered about 1812. The abraded scenes include an arch supporting an equestrian statue, two free-standing columns and other structures. On other examples, inscriptions identify the setting as Baiae, an exclusive resort on the Bay of Naples. The bottle may have been made at Pozzuoli, also on the Bay of Naples, a known glassmaking centre in Roman times. Late 3rd to early 4th century AD. H. 18.4 cm. Corning Museum of Glass, 62.1.31.

Above Cage cups with openwork decoration are the most luxurious glasses made in the later Roman Empire. Strictly speaking, 'cup' is a misnomer because openwork occurs on beakers, bowls and other forms, including this hanging lamp. Controversy surrounds the method used to create the openwork, although most agree that the task was completed by grinding and polishing. Provenance unknown, early 4th century AD. Diam. 12.1 cm. Corning Museum of Glass, 87.1.1.

by shallow facets, were made in the city. A group of bottles with wheel-abraded decoration showing prominent buildings at Baiae and Puteoli (Pozzuoli) on the Bay of Naples, Italy, were presumably made in or near Pozzuoli. Finally, segmental bowls with scratch-engraved scenes were produced in the glassmaking centres on the River Rhine.

Cage cups

Cage cups, the rarest and most luxurious late Roman glass vessels, are objects with finely carved openwork decoration, that is ornament with patterns of holes. In most cases, the object (most often a beaker or a bowl) is surrounded by a 'cage' attached to the wall by well-concealed supports. The cage may be accompanied by an openwork Greek or Latin inscription. One inscription, on a beaker found at Strasbourg, France, in 1825, names Emperor Maximian (r. AD 286–310), suggesting that the object was either a gift to the emperor or a present from him to a member of his court. The base glass of these cups is usually colourless but occasionally the cages and inscriptions are enlivened with bands of colour. The most remarkable cage

cup of all, however, known as the Lycurgus Cup, is made entirely of dichroic
glass – that is, glass that appears to change colour (it is green when seen
in reflected light and red when light shines through it). Although earlier
examples exist, most cage cups were made in the third and fourth centuries
AD. They were luxury objects admired for the virtuosity of the master
craftsmen who made them, although why they were fashionable at this time
and not others remains unknown.

Painted and enamelled glass
Between the first and fourth centuries AD, the Romans also decorated
glass with enamel, cold-painting, combinations of paint and gilding and
occasionally unprotected gold foil (see p. 13 for a note on these techniques).
Among the earliest enamelled objects are drinking vessels decorated with
humans, animals and vegetation. The form is known as a Hofheim cup,

Right The 'Paris Plate' depicts the story of Paris, who was asked by Zeus to judge which of three goddesses – Hera, Athena and Aphrodite – was the most beautiful. The plate was reverse-painted: that is, it was intended to be seen through the glass and so details were painted first and the background was painted afterwards. Found in Syria, 3rd to 4th century. Diam. 21 cm. Corning Museum of Glass, 55.1.85.

Below The 'Daphne Ewer' is cold-painted and gilded. It illustrates the story of Daphne, whose name means 'laurel' in Greek. Fleeing from the unwanted attention of Apollo, Daphne was saved by turning into a laurel tree. The ewer was found at Kerch in the Crimea. Eastern Mediterranean, probably Syria, late 2nd or early 3rd century. H. 22.2 cm. Corning Museum of Glass, 55.1.86.

Opposite This gold glass roundel is decorated with a rural scene of a shepherd holding pan-pipes and guarding his flock. Originally the centre of a dish or bowl, the fragment has been carefully trimmed for reuse, probably as a marker in one of the catacombs of Rome. Rome, 4th century. Diam. 9.7 cm. Corning Museum of Glass, 66.1.37, formerly in the Sangiorgi collection.

after a prolific find-place in Germany. Enamelled cups of this type were made for a short period in the first century, perhaps between about AD 40 and 60. A handful of later Roman objects have reverse-painted ornament. Despite its poor state of preservation, the most accomplished reverse-painted object is the third- to fourth-century Paris Plate, so-called because it depicts the Judgment of Paris, an episode in Greek mythology (pictured above).

Gold glass

Gold glasses are objects decorated with gold sandwiched between two fused layers of glass, most of which date from the third and the fourth centuries. Roman glassworkers applied the gold as foil and created designs by removing unwanted areas, such as the background, and adding details by scratching or painting. The most common Roman gold glasses are roundels with a wide variety of themes, including Old Testament subjects, Christ and saints, Jewish subjects, pagan deities and portraits. Many examples were found in Roman catacombs, where they were set in plaster surrounding niches used for burying the dead. It was once thought that the roundels are complete objects, but today we know that they were made from the centres of dishes and bowls, thanks to the discovery of several gold glass vessels with foot rings and parts of the side of the vessel still attached.

Europe between Rome and the Renaissance

In AD 286, Emperor Diocletian (r. 284–305) reorganized the government of the Roman Empire. He increased the number of provinces and gave responsibility to two emperors (he was one of them), each with a junior colleague, with a well-defined area of authority. The new arrangement soon evolved into two virtually independent realms, a division formally recognized in 340. In the Eastern Empire, Constantine I (r. 306–337) made Constantinople (modern Istanbul) the permanent capital. Usually known as the Byzantine Empire, the eastern realm attained its greatest extent under Emperor Justinian (r. 527–565), who conquered many of the provinces of the Western Empire, including Italy. The Byzantine Empire contracted in the seventh century, when Arab armies overran the rich provinces of Syria and Egypt, but survived until 1453, when it was conquered by the Ottoman Turks.

In the Western Empire nations from outside the frontier occupied the former Roman provinces in the fifth and sixth centuries, establishing small, independent kingdoms. Rome, 'the eternal city,' was sacked in 410. From then on, cities and long-distance trade declined throughout the former Western Empire. Almost everyone lived in rural communities and almost all social and economic life was local.

Western Europe revived in the later Middle Ages. The population expanded and economic surpluses fuelled the growth of cities. Wealth generated patronage and encouraged investment in trade. A new society emerged, with power in the hands of inherited aristocracy and the newly rich, and a growing class of craftsmen and traders. Despite the ravages of the Black Death, which killed one-third of the population in the fourteenth century, late medieval Europe prospered. Glassmakers produced useful objects in unprecedented quantities, while those who could afford it imported spectacular glasses from the Islamic world.

Below The 'Aldrevandin Beaker', Venice, c.1330. Some scholars believe that Venetians learned the technique of enamelling on glass from the Byzantine world, as three of the five painters on glass, known to have been active in Venice in the 13th century, came from Zadar in Croatia and Navplion in Greece, two Byzantine cities conquered by the Venetians in 1202 and 1204. Other scholars point to the magnificent enamelled glass produced in Syria and advocate an Islamic origin. H. 13 cm. British Museum, 1876,1104.3.

Medieval glass in Western Europe

Despite the upheavals of the fifth and sixth centuries, remnants of the Roman glass industry survived and some of the earliest medieval glasses resemble those produced by late Roman glassmakers. Drinking horns and claw beakers, for example, were made in Roman Germany and the beakers themselves were made continuously until the seventh or eighth century.

In the later Middle Ages, the most refined glass tableware in southern Germany, Switzerland and parts of Italy was either colourless or almost colourless; it was the forerunner of the Venetian *cristallo* glass of the Renaissance. This colourless glass was made by carefully selecting the raw materials and by adding manganese, a mineral known as 'glassmakers' soap', because it counteracts the colours caused by impurities.

The most widely discussed medieval fine tableware consists of a group of enamelled vessels known as the 'Aldrevandin Beakers'. They take their name from the example in the British Museum, which bears the inscription 'MAGISTER . ALDREVANDIN . ME . FECI[T]': ('Master Aldrevandin made me'). Almost every large-scale excavation in Germany or Switzerland produces Aldrevandin fragments from the late thirteenth and early fourteenth centuries. Their Latin inscriptions and the style of decoration, which includes Christian saints and coats of arms, are emphatically European. At this date, on the other hand, enamelling on glass was unknown elsewhere in Europe. So there is still the question: were the decorators of the these vessels influenced by ornament in the Islamic world or in Byzantium?

Finds from archaeological excavations also show that most medieval domestic vessels were intended for serving and consuming beverages, and contemporary paintings of the Last Supper, the Marriage at Cana and Herod's Feast depict tables set with bottles of wine and a large number of glass beakers or goblets. The beakers are either plain, or have applied ornament or patterns made by inflating the molten glass in a mould. The

Right This 'Hedwig Beaker' is so-called because two similar objects are associated with the legend of Saint Hedwig. Born in 1174, Hedwig was an ascetic woman, who married the Duke of Silesia. The duke enjoyed an extravagant lifestyle and he criticized his wife for her austere habits, which included drinking water instead of wine. One day, he snatched a glass of water from her, only to find that it had been transformed into wine. Hedwig retired to a convent, where she died in 1243. Twenty-four years later, the pope proclaimed her a saint. The beaker was blown and wheel-cut, perhaps at Palermo, Italy, in the 12th century. H. 14 cm. British Museum, 1959,0414.1, donated by Brooke Sewell.

Left Despite the social, political and economic dislocation that accompanied the end of the Roman Empire, glassmaking in Germany continued without interruption. Among the forms made both before and after the collapse of Roman rule were drinking horns. Horns like this example, made from translucent olive green glass and decorated with trails, were made along the middle and lower Rhine in the 4th and 5th centuries. Bingerbrück, Germany, 5th century. L. 34 cm. British Museum, 1873,0502.212, bequeathed by Felix Slade.

beakers with mould-blown decoration usually have an overall pattern of ribs or lozenges. The ornament on beakers with applied decoration may consist of 'prunts' (blobs of glass attached to the side of the beaker), horizontal trails or vertical ribs. These objects represent something new in the repertoire of European glassware, which was now more widely available than at any time since the end of the Roman Empire.

But the importance of glass was not confined solely to the domestic sphere. In the twelfth and thirteenth centuries, Latin translations of books written by ancient Greek and medieval Muslim scientists began to circulate in Europe. Students in two fields of this new knowledge benefitted directly from recent improvements in European glassmaking: science and medicine. Many scientific experiments depended on glass apparatus that was transparent and did not contaminate its contents by corroding. No apparatus played a more important role in medieval experiments than the still, used for preparing acids used in alchemy and for distilling alcohol.

In medicine, physicians used glass apparatus to prepare substances for treating ailments, and they took advantage of the transparency of glass flasks for uroscopy – that is, observing the colour of urine to diagnose disease. And in 1268, Roger Bacon (c.1220–92) recorded this remarkable observation: 'If the letters of a book are viewed through a segment of a sphere . . . they will appear far better and larger'. The segment of a sphere is a lens and reading glasses consist of a pair of lenses. Spectacles, worn on the nose like a pince-nez, were invented in Italy not long afterwards. Spectacles were a brilliant innovation and for more than seven hundred years the lives of countless millions of people have been transformed by their glass lenses.

Despite the perfection of colourless glass for scientific equipment and lenses, most late medieval glass produced in central and northern Europe was formed of green 'forest glass'. This was made in small glasshouses located in forests, which provided a convenient source of fuel and potash, the flux which lowered the temperature at which sand melts. The repertoire of forest glass consists mainly of vessels for drinking: mould-blown and prunted beakers, tall, narrow *Stangengläser* (narrow cylindrical vessels, hence their German name, which means 'pole glass'), and bottles for pouring or storing liquid. A late variety of prunted beaker was a vessel known as a *Krautstrunk* ('cabbage stalk'). The name is appropriate: the ornament consists of large prunts that project from the side of the vessel like the scars on a cabbage stalk after the leaves have been removed.

Stoking furnaces and making potash consumed trees on a scale that alarmed the authorities, who were already anxious because another industry made even greater demands on the resources of Europe's forests. As the population grew and cities expanded, the construction industry flourished and required timber on an unprecedented scale. Something had to be done, and in the fourteenth and fifteenth centuries the consumption of wood was controlled. In the forests of the Spessart Mountains in Germany, regulations limited the quantities of glass that could be produced. In England, the problem reached crisis proportions, when the navy feared that deforestation would make it impossible to find timber for building ships. In 1615, by Royal Proclamation, glassmakers were prohibited from burning wood and compelled to use coal instead.

Byzantine glassmaking

Unlike our knowledge of medieval glass in Western Europe, we know extraordinarily little about the glass vessels made in the Byzantine Empire. Even in Constantinople, the glass found in excavations so far has failed to live up to the promise held out by literary references in written sources, which list conical glasses, bowls, dishes, platters, jars and cups. The treasury of Saint Mark's Cathedral in Venice, however, preserves a number of glass vessels brought from Constantinople in 1204. They include a purple bowl richly decorated with gilding, silver-stain and enamel. Comparable ornament occurs on Byzantine ivories of the tenth and eleventh centuries, and there is little doubt that the bowl, too, is Byzantine and of a similar date. The same date has been suggested for several fragments of silver-stained vessels, and for glass bracelets with silver-stained or enamelled decoration from the Balkan region of eastern Europe. The vessels are rare examples of the luxury glass produced in Byzantium in around 1000.

In fact, the aspect of Byzantine glassmaking about which we know most is the production of *tesserae*, the cubes of coloured glass used in mosaics. Many millions of *tesserae* were required for the mosaics that covered the walls and ceilings of Byzantine churches and (to a much more limited extent) for the icons known as 'micro-mosaics'. Mosaicists from Constantinople were in demand even outside the Byzantine Empire. Caliph Hakam II (r. 961–976) employed them to decorate the Great Mosque at Cordoba in southern Spain, while in Ukraine, Prince Vladimir (r. *c.*978–1015) imported Byzantine craftsmen to build and decorate with mosaics the Church of the Tithe in his capital, Kiev.

Our knowledge of Byzantine glass of the twelfth and thirteenth centuries is somewhat better. In the twelfth century a German monk, Theophilus (probably a pseudonym), recorded that 'Greeks' made gilded and enamelled glass. It seems likely that Theophilus was referring to bottles and other objects made of dark blue and other coloured glasses, which do have gilded and enamelled decoration. The most common form is a cylindrical bottle with a narrow neck. The decoration consists of foliate motifs, birds, animals and geometric elements. All these objects are closely similar and it seems likely that they were made at one place in one relatively short period. The best evidence for where and when these objects were produced has been found in Cyprus. Finds from the castle known as Saranda Kolones, at Paphos, indicate that glass of this type was in use from sometime after 1191 until 1222, when the castle was destroyed. Human figures on a bottle from Nicosia, also in Cyprus, resemble figures on thirteenth-century Cypriot pottery and suggest that the glasses were made on the island.

Opposite Two beakers decorated with gilded and enamelled roundels containing birds. They belong to a group of vessels found mostly in the eastern Mediterranean, although examples have been found as far afield as Sweden, the United Kingdom and Belarus. Made in the Byzantine Empire or Cyprus, late 12th or early 13th century. H. (taller beaker) 22.3 cm. Corning Museum of Glass, 67.1.19 and 67.1.20.

The Islamic world and Eastern Asia

The Islamic world began to take shape in the seventh century AD. When the Prophet Muhammad died in 632, he was scarcely known outside the Arabian peninsula. Twenty years later, Arab armies had devoured the empires of Byzantium and the Sasanians. In 640, the Byzantines relinquished Palestine and Syria; in 642, they surrendered Egypt. Nine years later, the Sasanians lost Iran and its neighbours. Within a century, Islam had tens of millions of followers from the Atlantic Ocean to the River Indus.

Over the years, the focus of power shifted: from Damascus to Baghdad, then to Cordoba, Cairo, Istanbul, Isfahan and Delhi. The distances that separate these cities – it is more than 4,600 miles from Cordoba to Delhi – underscore the fact that the Islamic world was, and still is, a vast area. But, despite the diversity of its inhabitants and cultures, in the Middle Ages this area was bound together by one religion (Islam), one legal system (Shari'a law, which governed the behaviour of the majority of the population), and one language for most business and administrative purposes (Arabic, the language of the Qur'an). Consequently, an 'international' vocabulary of the visual arts emerged, based on geometrical and vegetal ornament and calligraphy, but always subject to local interpretations.

The earliest Islamic glass
In the first two centuries after the Arab conquest, glassmakers in the Islamic realm built on local traditions. In the Syro-Palestinian region, for example, they adopted the glass tube the Romans had used for cosmetics, but adapted it in an entirely new way. The tube was reduced in size and placed on the back of a glass camel made by manipulating hot glass and adorning it with trails. These 'dromedary flasks' became extremely popular, and examples have been found in Egypt, Syria, Iraq and Iran.

In Egypt, glassmakers experimented with pincered and stamped decoration. The former was made by pinching the hot glass with tongs, the jaws of which were decorated with patterns that include inscriptions and zoomorphic motifs. The most common variety of stamped glass consists of 'coin weights', which were produced in huge numbers in and after the eighth century, and of 'vessel stamps', which guaranteed the capacity of vessels used for weighing and measuring.

Islamic glass: ninth to eleventh centuries

By the ninth century products ranged from utilitarian vessels, some of which have applied or mould-blown ornament, to exquisite luxury items. Numerous vessels were decorated by blowing the glass into moulds, a technique which allowed the glassblower to make decorated objects almost as quickly as plain ones. Simple patterns were produced in dip moulds, while complex ornament, with birds, animals, foliage and inscriptions, was made in full-size moulds consisting of two pieces joined by hinges.

Some of the more elaborate objects made between the ninth and eleventh centuries were finished by cold-working, either by engraving or cutting on the wheel. The engraved objects were scratched with a hand-held tool tipped with a splinter of very hard stone. They consist of vessels decorated with geometric or vegetal motifs, sometimes accompanied by inscriptions. The earliest scratch-engraved glasses, made in Egypt or the Middle East, were produced in the eighth century. Several examples were

Above Made in Iran between the 12th and 14th centuries, this pitcher was decorated by inflating a bubble of molten glass in a tumbler-shaped dip mould. The rim and neck were made from a separate gather and the two parts were then reheated and fused. This type of mould-blown glass is often attributed to the Gurgan region of northern Iran. H. 16.2 cm. Corning Museum of Glass, 66.1.5.

Right In the 8th and 9th centuries, glassworkers in the Syro-Palestinian region and Egypt decorated objects by engraving them with tools mounted with chips of stone with a hardness of more than 7 on the Mohs scale: for example, topaz. Islamic scratch-engraved glasses were highly prized, and examples were concealed in the crypt of the Famen Temple in China, in 874. H. 20.7 cm. Corning Museum of Glass, 68.1.1.

Right To create this object, the glassworker blew a paper-thin bubble of colourless glass and cased it with an equally delicate layer of green. The blank was entrusted to a glass cutter, who removed most of the overlay with rotating wheels fed with abrasive and perhaps hand tools. The result is a scene outlined in green with lines so fluid that they appear almost calligraphic. Known as the 'Corning Ewer', this small masterpiece was made in Western Asia or Egypt, *c.*1000. H. 16 cm. Corning Museum of Glass, 85.1.1.

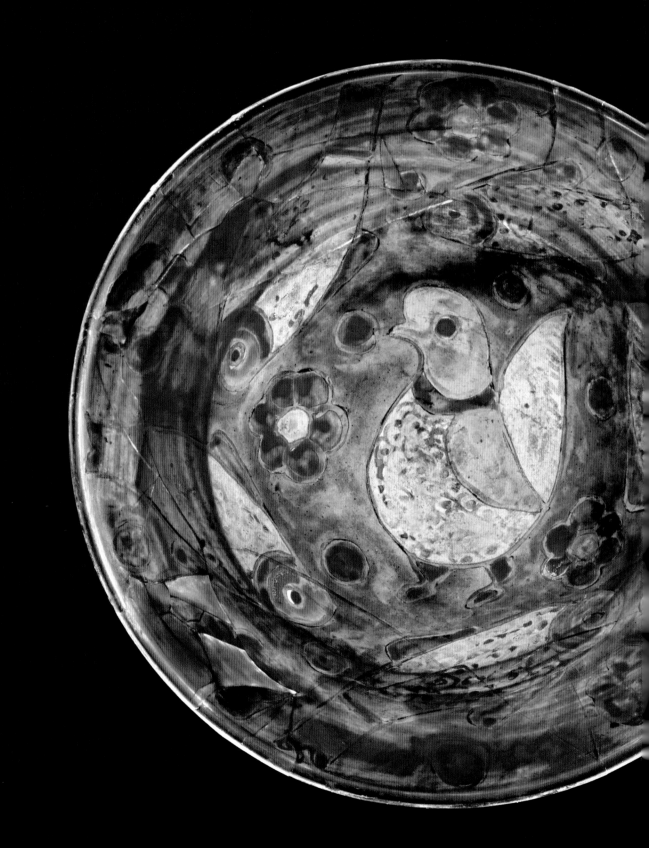

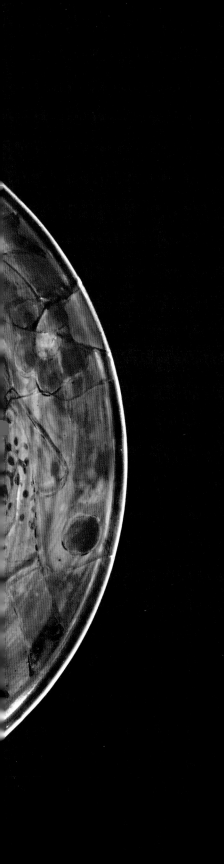

placed in the crypt of the pagoda at the Famen Temple in China, in 874. Small quantities of Islamic glass, carried along the so-called Silk Route, arrived in China as items of trade and perhaps also as gifts. The Famen Temple finds, together with finds from tombs elsewhere in China, provide valuable fixed points in the chronology of scratch-engraved and other Islamic glassware.

Islamic glass workers made extensive use of the technique of wheel-cutting, which had been practised by the Romans and Sasanians. Between the ninth and eleventh centuries, the technique was used to produce some of the finest masterpieces of Islamic glass. Many wheel-cut vessels had linear ornament or were decorated in the 'bevelled' style, in which outlines are cut on a slant and there is no distinct plane forming the background. The most refined objects were relief-cut: that is, the entire background was excavated, leaving the outlines of the ornament and some details in low relief.

Most early Islamic relief-cut glasses were made from colourless blanks that imitated rock crystal. However, a few coloured examples are known, in green, turquoise and purple. Glass cutters also decorated blanks made with the cameo technique, in which a layer of glass of one colour is applied to an object of a different colour. Subsequently, most of the outer layer is removed, leaving the ornament in relief on a different-coloured background (Islamic cameo glass usually has coloured decoration on a colourless ground). Cameo glass had been made by the Romans, but there is no reason to suppose that production persisted into the Islamic period; presumably, the technique was rediscovered in Western Asia or Egypt in the ninth century.

Left The technique of painting glass with metallic stains was discovered in the Islamic world in the 8th century. Silver and copper, used singly or together, produced different colours, as on this bowl made in Egypt in the 9th century. The bird is surrounded by a circle of five fish. Diam. 15.8 cm. Corning Museum of Glass, 99.1.1.

Right In the 9th and 10th centuries, glassmakers in the Near East made a small number of drinking vessels and bottles (such as that shown here) decorated with gold or silver foil sandwiched between two fused layers of glass. Although the technique recalls Roman gold glasses, there is no evidence to suggest that it was practised continuously between the 4th and the 9th centuries. Syria, 9th–10th century. H. 14.5 cm. British Museum, 1978,1011.2.

An entirely different variety of decorated glass was painted with metallic stain. This technique, which appears to have been discovered in Egypt or Syria in the eighth century, was obtained by painting the surface with a mixture of sulphur and finely powdered copper and/or silver oxide suspended in an acidic medium such as vinegar, then firing the object in oxygen-free conditions at a temperature of about 600°C (1112°F). The temperature was insufficient to soften the glass and cause the object to collapse, but high enough to cause the absorption of the metal into the glass, thereby creating a stain, which may be brown, yellow, green or red.

Two other varieties of decorated glass produced in the ninth and tenth centuries were mosaic glass and gold glass. Islamic mosaic glass is rare. Surviving objects include plates, cups and perfume bottles, many of which are formed from slices of 'bull's eye' canes, which are so-called because they have a concentric pattern surrounding a central dot. Mosaic glass tiles adorned part of the Jawsaq al-Khāqāni, the palace built by Caliph al-Mu'tasim between 836 and 842 at Samarra in Iraq. Gold glass is even rarer and only a handful of objects are known to exist. Two of these objects have Arabic inscriptions, which resemble the script in ninth- and tenth-century manuscripts, and this allows us to place Islamic gold glasses in that period.

In the eleventh and twelfth centuries, some of the most distinctive Islamic utilitarian glassware included bottles, bowls, sprinklers, bird shaped vessels and gaming pieces formed from coloured glass and decorated with opaque white trails, which were marvered (rolled to and fro on a smooth surface) until they were flush with the surface side of the vessel. The most popular colours for the base glass were purple, blue and green. Sometimes, a mass of glass on the end of the blowpipe was decorated with trails and then inflated in a mould to produce a ribbed effect, or featherlike designs were made by manipulating the trails. A few objects

Opposite This canteen is among the most magnificent Islamic gilded and enamelled glasses. It is decorated with arabesques, birds and human figures: horsemen, a female musician and a male drinking wine. Their clothing and helmets identify the riders as Christians and it is difficult to understand who might have commissioned the object. Made in Syria or Egypt, 1250–60. H. 22.5 cm. British Museum, 1869,0120.3, bequeathed by Felix Slade.

Above The 'Durighello Bottle' (named after its first known owner, the collector Joseph-Ange Durighello) is an outstanding example of 13th-century glass decorated with spiral trails which, while the glass was semi-molten, were dragged up and down with a pointed tool to produce a featherlike pattern. The bottle is said to come from Adana in south-east Turkey. H. 20 cm. British Museum, 1913,0522.39.

Right The most impressive Islamic glass of the 13th and 14th centuries was decorated with gilding and multicoloured enamels. On this hanging lamp, the goblet on the shield shows that it belonged to the sultan's cup bearer, a high official at the Mamlūk court. One of the inscriptions gives the cup bearer's name. He is known to have served Sultan Qalāūn (r. 1293–1341) and this information allows us to date the lamp. H. 33 cm. British Museum, 1869,0624.1, bequeathed by Felix Slade.

are also gilded. Vessels of this type were made in the Near East and Egypt.

At the same time, monochrome glass with mould-blown decoration continued to be made. Among the best known objects of this period are bottles, jugs and other vessels of coloured glass reputedly from northern Iran. The decoration includes dip-moulded ribs and honeycomb or lattice motifs, and vegetal ornament and inscriptions.

Islamic glass: twelfth to fifteenth centuries

The most spectacular Islamic glass of the period between the twelfth and fifteenth centuries has gilded and enamelled ornament. The canteen on page 57, for example, is decorated with hunters on horseback, a female musician, a man drinking, animals, birds and elaborate scrollwork. The gold was painted on the glass as a fine suspension, after which it was fired at a low temperature. Decorative details were scratched in the gold with a stylus. The enamel consisted of powdered glass which was applied in

The gilded and enamelled ornament on this set of bottles shows that they were decorated in Gujarat on the west coast of India, in the first half of the 18th century. The shape of the bottles originated in Europe, and it is likely that some decorated vessels were imported while others were made locally. The gold funnel was used to fill the bottles. H. (all) 13 cm. Corning Museum of Glass, 2002.1.1.

the form of paste and fused by attaching the object to a pontil (an iron rod on which the molten glass is worked) and heating it in the mouth of the furnace. Most – perhaps all – twelfth- to fifteenth-century Islamic gilded and enamelled glass was made in Syria and Egypt. Some of the earliest objects are decorated with figural and architectural scenes, the style of which suggests that they were produced in northern Syria in the early thirteenth century. After about 1250, figural scenes declined in popularity and were replaced by heraldic devices and, later, by lotus blossoms, phoenixes and motifs of Chinese origin. In the fourteenth century, forms included bottles, basins, jugs, beakers and cups. Hanging lamps, used to illuminate mosques and other buildings, survive in relatively large numbers.

Islamic glass: sixteenth to eighteenth centuries
Later decorative glass made in the Islamic world seldom matched the quality of the finest creations of the tenth to fourteenth centuries. The invasion of central and Western Asia by the Mongols, which culminated in the conquest of Baghdad in 1258, seriously disrupted urban life and industry, including glassmaking. After a partial recovery, the entire region was devastated again, by Timur (1336–1405), who invaded Iran in 1383 and India in 1398. In western Asia, the glass industry never fully recovered, and from then on the wealthy imported their glassware from Europe. The period, often called the Age of Empires, was dominated by three great dynasties: the Ottomans (1281–1923), the Safavids (1501–1732) and the Mughals (1526–1858). From a modest realm in Anatolia, the Ottomans captured Constantinople (Istanbul) in 1453 and went on to create an empire that encompassed most of North Africa, the Arabian peninsula and parts of eastern Europe; the Safavids ruled Iran; and the Mughals ruled much of the Indian subcontinent.

Despite documentary evidence for glassmaking at Istanbul during the reigns of Bayezid II (1481–1512) and Süleymān the Magnificent (1520–66), not a single object has been reliably attributed to Ottoman glassmakers before the late eighteenth century, when a factory at Beykoz near Istanbul began to make high-quality glass that rivalled the objects imported from Venice and Bohemia. Similarly, although seventeenth-century travellers noted the existence of glasshouses at Isfahan and Shiraz, very few examples of Iranian glass vessels are known before the eighteenth century, when elegant 'swan's neck' rosewater bottles, some of which were free-blown and others decorated in moulds, became common. Apart from bangles and utilitarian objects, most of the glass used in Mughal India was imported, although local craftsmen added ornament by cutting, gilding or enamelling.

Square 'case bottles', for example, originally imported from Germany or the Low Countries and perhaps copied in India, were decorated with gilded and enamelled scenes of courtly life, flowers and foliage.

Eastern Asia

Glassmaking in the Far East began later than in Western Asia and we know little about glass in China before the early Qing dynasty (1644–1911). Evidently, jade, ceramics and lacquer appealed to Chinese taste more strongly than glass. Even so, the late introduction of glass is surprising because Chinese bronze founders were casting objects of great complexity by about 1500 BC and potters began to make high-fired ceramics some two centuries later. For hundreds of years, however, this mastery of high-temperature furnace technology was not applied to glassmaking and the earliest securely dated glass beads belong to the Western Zhou dynasty, who ruled between the eleventh and the eighth centuries BC. Rather more beads and other small objects were produced in the Spring and Autumn Period (770–476 BC) and the period of the Warring States (475–221 BC). Of slightly

later date are two cast glass cups and a plate from the tomb of Liu Sheng (d. 113 BC) in Hebei province. Other objects made during the Han dynasty (206 BC–AD 220) include beads, belt hooks, inlays, perforated discs known as *bi*, and pieces of glass garments (perforated rectangular and circular elements intended to be stitched together).

Although we are not sure how it came about, glass-blowing was introduced in the course of the next few centuries and locally made blown glass objects, as well as imports from the Roman and Sasanian empires, have been found in tombs. Many of these objects are of translucent green glass imitating jade, a gemstone particularly sought after in China.

Little is known about glassmaking in China during the Song (960–1279), Yuan (1280–1368) or Ming (1368–1644) dynasties, although in 1982 the remains of a fourteenth-century glass factory were discovered at Zibo (formerly Boshan) in Shandong province. The find included the remains of some twenty furnaces, together with waste glass, pots and small objects.

Chinese glassmaking underwent a profound change in the early Qing period, during the reign of Emperor Kangxi (1662–1722), who in 1689 established an imperial workshop in Beijing. Jesuit missionaries, such as Kilian Stumpf (1655–1720), provided much of the expertise to set up the Palace Workshop, which by 1696 was supplying lenses for telescopes at the imperial observatory. By the beginning of the eighteenth century, the workshop made snuff bottles and other objects in a wide range of colours, sometimes with enamelled decoration. In addition to plain and enamelled glassware, Chinese craftsmen produced a large quantity of cameo glass with floral and, in a few cases, figural decoration.

Glassmaking spread from China to Japan and Korea. In both countries, the earliest locally made objects were beads and pendants, including composite eye beads and cast comma-shaped pendants known as *magatama* in Japan and *kogok* in Korea. In Japan, bead making began in the mid-Yayoi period (about 300 BC–AD 300), while in Korea, the earliest beads are attributed to the period of the Three Kingdoms (57 BC–AD 668). Imported glass vessels occur in both countries. Small blown-glass vessels were also made locally at this time. In Japan, glassmaking was not practised on a large scale until the Edo period (1600–1868). A Japanese translation of a compendium of European texts about glassmaking, published in 1810, encouraged the development of the glass industry which, in the second half of the nineteenth century, manufactured pressed glass and brilliant wheel-cut glass in imitation of European and American products. The industrial production of glassware in Korea began at an even later date.

Opposite Two decanters and three *sake* cups on a stand, made in Japan, c.1857. The cups were used in the *sakazuki* ceremony of affirming loyalty. They represent heaven (at the top), earth and humankind. At traditional weddings, the bride and groom take turns sipping *sake* (rice wine) three times from each cup. Diam. (largest cup) 11 cm. Corning Museum of Glass, 55.6.18.

Renaissance and modern Europe, 1450–1900

By the fifteenth century, glassmakers in northern Italy routinely produced thin-walled colourless or almost colourless glass, known as *cristallo*. The glassmakers of late medieval Venice played a prominent role in this industry. By 1224, they had formed a guild, an association of people practising the same trade or craft. The government repeatedly asserted control over the city's guilds and in 1291, in order to increase its control and reduce the risk of fire, the Grand Council decreed that the glassmakers had to transfer their activities to the nearby island of Murano.

The success of the late medieval Venetian glass industry was due in part to the use of raw materials of unusual purity. Although sand was available locally, by 1332 Venetian glassmakers imported quartz pebbles from the mainland. For superior soda, they went farther afield: to Syria and Egypt. A Venetian document of 1255 refers to plant ash from Alexandria. But by the end of that century Syrian plant ash was the preferred source of soda and in the early fourteenth century its use became mandatory, as part of the government's efforts to preserve the high quality of Venetian glass.

The Venetians also imported broken glass for recycling. In glassmaking, the addition of a small quantity of crushed glass facilitates the process of melting the raw materials, and for this reason broken glass was traded. Records show that the importation of broken glass dates from 1233. It was of great importance to Venetian glassmakers and in 1277, an agreement between the doge of Venice, Jacopo Contarini, and the prince of Antioch, Bohemond VII, exempted Venetians from paying duty in the port of Tripoli (in present-day Lebanon), except when they exported broken glass.

Glassmaking in Venice, 1450–1700

In the mid- and later 1400s, the repertoire of Venetian glassmakers exploded like a magnificent display of fireworks. The sudden pre-eminence of fine

This exquisitely gilded and enamelled glass is known as the 'Behaim Beaker'. It is decorated with the arms of the Behaim family of Nuremberg, Germany, Archangel Michael slaying Satan in the form of a dragon, and Saint Catherine of Alexandria. The combination of Saint Michael and Saint Catherine is very unusual. It probably refers to the marriage, on 7 July 1495, of Michael Behaim, a Nuremberg patrician, and Catherine Lochner, the daughter of a rich merchant. Venice, probably 1495. H. 10.7 cm. Corning Museum of Glass, 84.3.24.

Below left Although this 'ring-handled' vase resembles tin-glazed earthenware produced in the Low Countries, it is made of opaque white *lattimo* glass. Possibly enamelled by the Venetian artist Giovanni-Maria Obizzo, the vase bears a portrait of King Henry VII of England (r. 1485–1509) and, on the other side, the king's personal device, a portcullis and chains. Venice, Italy, c.1500. H. 19.8 cm. British Museum, 1979,0401.1.

Below right This goblet depicts two pairs of lovers and so probably celebrates the engagement or marriage of two unidentified aristocrats. The goblet was made in three parts: the light blue bowl and foot imitate turquoise, while the darker stem resembles lapis lazuli. Like the ring-handled vase pictured alongside, the goblet may have been decorated by Giovanni-Maria Obizzo. Venice, Italy, c.1500. H. 18.9 cm. British Museum, WB.55, bequeathed by Baron Ferdinand Anselm de Rothschild.

Venetian glass is associated with the name of Angelo Barovier, who appeared first in a document of 1424 and who died in 1460. Barovier was a legend in his own lifetime: in 1455, he was in Milan, where he impressed Duke Francesco Sforza (1401–66) with his fine colourless *cristallo*. Four years later, he visited Florence and there, too, he won praise for his glass. His fame extended to Naples and the court of King Alfonso V. When he died, Ludovico Carbone described him as the very best maker of *cristallo*.

Cristallo is the only type of glass associated with Angelo Barovier, but documents record other products made in Murano in the fifteenth century. In 1470–71, Pietro di Giorgio was described as a '*maistro da dora a smaltar lavorieri de vero*' (a master of gilding and enamelling glassware) and in 1490 Giovanni Maria Obizzo was named as the painter of more than one thousand pieces of *lattimo* (a translucent white glass resembling porcelain) and other coloured glasses. Thus, by the end of the fifteenth century, Venetian glassmakers produced colourless glass that imitated rock crystal (hence the name *cristallo*), *lattimo* (latte is the Italian word for milk),

other coloured glasses and gilded and enamelled decoration. Some of the most magnificent Venetian glasses made between about 1470 and 1550 are elaborately decorated with gold foil and polychrome enamel.

Like *cristallo*, several of the coloured glasses manufactured in the late fifteenth and sixteenth centuries also resembled precious or semi-precious stones, such as emerald, sapphire, turquoise, opal and chalcedony. This is not surprising because, in addition to glass vessels and huge quantities of beads, Venetian glassmakers had produced imitations of gemstones for at least two centuries. Indeed, when the government removed the glassmakers from the city to the island of Murano in 1291, the makers of false gems were allowed to stay in Venice itself. Their furnaces were small and they presented little risk of fire. In 1500 Marcantonio Coccio Sabellico reported that 'there is no kind of precious stone which cannot be imitated by . . . the [Venetian] glassworkers'.

Sabellico also described a glass sphere decorated with 'all sorts of flowers which clothe the meadows in spring', a clear reference to *millefiori* ('a thousand flowers') or mosaic glass. Unlike glassmakers in ancient

Right *Calcedonio* (chalcedony) was one of the imitations of hardstones perfected by Venetian glassmakers in the 15th century. The bowls on the left and at the centre were made about 1500; the outside of the smaller vessel has applied ornament making the diamond pattern known as '*nipt diamond waies*.' The late 17th-century tankard is speckled with metallic copper inclusions. H. (tankard) 18 cm. British Museum, 1878,1230.266.

Below This covered beaker was made in Venice or at a glasshouse elsewhere in Europe where Venetian-style glass was produced. The glass imitates a semi-precious stone, opal, which often has a milky appearance with flashes of brilliant colour. The beaker, blown in a three-part mould, depicts a triumphant procession of marine deities. 16th or 17th century. H. 23.5 cm. British Museum, WB.56, bequeathed by Baron Ferdinand Anselm de Rothschild.

times, who made mosaic glass by fusing slices of canes with patterned cross sections, the Venetians did not fuse the slices but attached them to bubbles of molten glass, which they then inflated to the desired size and shape.

Canes were also employed to make various kinds of *vetro a filigrana* (filigree glass). Whereas mosaic glass incorporates slices of canes, *filigrana* is decorated with lengths of cane, which are usually of opaque white glass or a combination of colourless *cristallo* and opaque white. The canes are laid side by side on a flat surface and carefully picked up on an elongated bubble of glass to produce a pattern that covers the entire vessel. *Vetro a fili* has a pattern of white stripes, in *vetro a retorti* (or a *retortoli*) the stripes are twisted, and in *vetro a reticello* superimposed canes produce a crisscross, net-like effect. All of these variants were in use by 1527, when a Murano glassmaker sought a patent to make *vetro a retortoli*.

One decorative technique that, unlike gilding and enamelling or *vetro a filigrana*, never achieved great popularity in Venice (or elsewhere in Italy) was engraving, although Vincenzo d'Angelo of the dal Gallo workshop was granted a patent to engrave glass in 1549. North of the Alps, however, engravers frequently decorated locally produced Venetian-style *cristallo* with delicate diamond-point engraving.

Traditionally, glassmakers' recipes were closely guarded secrets. Thus, the publication in 1612 of Antonio Neri's *L'Arte Vetraria* ('*The Art of Glassmaking*') must have shocked glassmakers all over Europe, for it contains 133 formulas for glass and glass-related materials from sources in his native Tuscany, and Venice and the Low Countries. In the course of the seventeenth century, translations of Neri's text, with additions, were printed in German, French, English and even Latin.

Opposite The decoration of this covered goblet consists of alternate canes of *vetro a fili* (plain stripes) and *vetro a retorti* (stripes with cable patterns). For each part of the goblet, the canes were picked up on a gather of colourless glass, which was then reheated and blown to the desired shape. Made in Venice or elsewhere at a factory that specialized in Venetian-style glassware. Late 16th or early 17th century. H. 34.9 cm. Corning Museum of Glass, 64.3.9.

By this time, the Venetians were no longer the only European makers of luxury glass, although factories on Murano continued to produce decorative glassware for an international market. In 1709, King Frederik IV of Denmark visited Venice and returned to Copenhagen with a large collection of glass vessels, which he installed in a special chamber adjoining the throne room at Rosenborg Castle.

European glassmaking 'in the manner of Venice', 1500–1700
All over Renaissance Europe, owning Venetian glass was regarded as a sign of wealth and sophistication. The transparency, brilliance, intricate forms, and even the fragility of Venetian glass fascinated consumers. However, the high cost of both transporting the glass and purchasing the pieces that arrived intact quickly led to a demand for local production.

It was not unusual for Venetian master glassmakers to receive tempting offers from foreign nobility and merchants. While the government of Venice made laws that restricted the emigration of glassmakers, it understood the commercial and diplomatic advantages of permitting short-term contracts abroad that did not endanger the city's own economic interests. At the same time, Venetian glassmakers were prepared to risk punishment at home by taking lucrative jobs abroad.

Consequently Venetian glassmakers helped to set up and manage workshops that made glass *à la façon de Venise* ('in the manner of Venice') in Austria, Spain, the Low Countries and England. Some of the local imitations of Venetian glass are so close to the originals that it is very difficult to distinguish one from the other. At other times, the glassmakers

used Venetian techniques to make shapes and ornament that appealed to local taste. In his drama *El Bandolero* (*The Bandit*), Tirso de Molina (*c.*1584–1648) described the distinctive Venetian-style glass made in north-east Spain: 'the Catalan nation competes with all others in Spain in the precision and skill of its crafts, such as its exquisite glasswares that rival those of Venice . . . although their peculiar differences and complexity of form mean that they cannot be confused with Venetian wares.'

It would be mistaken to assume that the use of Venetian and Venetian-style glass was always confined to the rich and famous. Archaeologists excavating the cesspit of a sixteenth-century tavern at Salzburg, Austria, found quantities of broken wine glasses that were either imported from Venice or made at Innsbruck or Hall.

Nevertheless, glassmaking enjoyed royal patronage in Austria. Ferdinand I, king of Hungary and Bohemia (r. 1526–64), and from 1558 emperor of the Holy Roman Empire, employed glassmakers to establish Venetian-style factories at Ljubljana in Slovenia; and in Austria at Hall, Innsbruck and Vienna in 1552. Ferdinand's second son, Ferdinand II (1529–95), archduke of the Austrian Empire, set up a private glasshouse at Innsbruck in 1570 and he is said to have tried his hand at making glass.

In France the royal family began to import Venetian glass in the fifteenth century. Some of the earliest closely datable Venetian or Venetian-style glasses from France are enamelled with the coat of arms of King Louis XII and Anne of Brittany, indicating that they were made some time between their marriage in 1499 and Anne's death in 1514. Excavations at the Louvre in Paris and elsewhere in France have revealed a wide variety of glass in the Italian style. Much of this glass was made by so-called Altarists, glassmakers from Altare in north-east Italy, who were working in Lyon as early as 1511. Their compatriots built workshops all over southern and central France. The most celebrated glassmaker in seventeenth-century France, Bernard Perrot (1617–1709), was born Bernardo Perrotto in Altare.

The manufacture of Venetian-style glass in the Low Countries began in the port-city of Antwerp (Belgium). In the sixteenth century, Antwerp was one of the greatest commercial cities in Europe. Italian merchants and bankers dominated the business community, Italian products were much in demand, and the city began to attract Italian craftsmen. Immigrant potters began to make Italian-style maiolica (tin-glazed earthenware) shortly after 1500, and in 1537 Lucas van Helmont was producing *verre cristallin l'instar de Venise* (*cristallo* glass imitating that of Venice). The first known Italian glassmaker working in Antwerp was a mirror-maker named Cornachini,

Right In classical mythology, Zeus took the form of a bull and abducted Europa, a beautiful mortal. This wafer-thin glass panel, engraved by Caspar Lehmann, illustrates the story. The crowned monogram is that of Christian II of Saxony and his wife Hedwig of Denmark. They married in 1602 and Christian died in 1611. Lehmann was employed by Christian between 1606 and 1608, and it is probable that the panel was engraved in Dresden, the capital of Saxony, during this period. H. 23 cm. Private collection, on loan to the British Museum.

Below Goblets with truncated conical bowls and gilded and enamelled ornament, which includes inscriptions in French, were made in France, perhaps by immigrant workers from Italy. Clothing, such as the costume and headdress worn by the woman on this example, suggests that the goblets were made in northern France or possibly the southern Netherlands, c.1530–60. H. 16.2 cm. British Museum, S.824, bequeathed by Felix Slade.

who in 1541 imported workers from Murano.

Across the North Sea, the use of glass in England increased in the sixteenth century, thanks to the imports from Venice and the Low Countries and the creation of a local glass industry. John Carré (d. 1572), a Frenchman who had worked in Antwerp, received a patent to make Venetian-style glass in London in 1567. His first workers were from the Low Countries, but in 1570 he hired two Venetians. One of the latter, Jacopo Verzelini, took over the glasshouse in 1572 and secured a twenty-one-year monopoly to make Venetian-style glass. Scholars attribute twelve remarkable glasses

to Verzelini, eleven of which have engraved decoration that is ascribed to Anthony de Lysle (active 1577–90), a Frenchman. Archaeological finds suggest that in Verzelini's day the use of glass in England was confined to wealthy households, unlike the situation in Austria at the same date.

Europe north of the Alps, 1600–1800
Cutting and engraving glass with stone or metal wheels had been practised in ancient times but, with the possible exception of Sicily, the method seems to have been lost in Europe in the Middle Ages. The technique was revived in central Europe at the end of the sixteenth century by engravers who took advantage of the hardness of Bohemian potash glass. Caspar Lehmann (c.1563–1623) was the first great glass engraver of modern times; he worked in Prague for the emperor Rudolf II, who appointed him to be the first Imperial Glass Engraver in 1608. After Lehman's death, the emperor appointed his pupil, Georg Schwandhart, to succeed him. Following Rudolf's precedent, European rulers became patrons of master engravers throughout the seventeenth and eighteenth centuries. Friedrich Winter

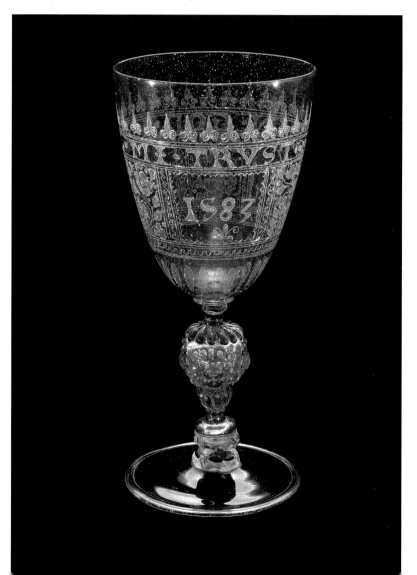

Right Between 1572 and 1592, Jacopo Verzelini produced Venetian-style glasses in a workshop at Crutched Friars, near the Tower of London, England. This goblet, dated 1583, is engraved with the motto of the Pewterers' Company of London: 'IN . GOD . IS . AL . MI . TRVST.' It is assumed, without proof, that the engraving was carried out by Anthony de Lysle, a Frenchman working in London at the time. H. 21 cm. Corning Museum of Glass, 63.2.8.

Left This diamond-point engraved dish is decorated on the rim with four oval cartouches containing emblems and mottos. At the centre, beneath the all-seeing eye of God, is a crowned monogram composed of two Gs, which is believed to refer to Gaston, Duke of Orléans (1608–60), son of Henry IV of France and younger brother of Louis XIII. France or the Low Countries, c.1640. Diam. 48.8 cm. Corning Museum of Glass, 77.3.34.

Below In the 17th century, the German city of Nuremberg was famous for the quality of its engraved glass. Glassmakers produced large goblets with tall stems made of distinctive bulbous knops separated by groups of paper-thin discs or 'mereses'. One such goblet (pictured here) is engraved with a portrait of Maximilian II, elector of Bavaria from 1679 to 1726. The portrait, signed by Wolfgang Schmidt, bears the date 1690. H. 34.9 cm. Corning Museum of Glass, 79.3.158.

(d. 1711), for example, another of the great names in the history of engraving, worked at Petersdorf, Germany, for Count von Schaffgotsch.

Schwandhart soon returned to Nuremburg, where glass engraving flourished throughout the seventeenth century. Some of the most notable vessels engraved are large covered goblets with straight-sided bowls and tall stems with distinctive hollow knops (see below). At the same time, Georg Schindler established a tradition of engraving glass at Dresden and Johann Hess introduced the technique at Frankfurt.

Although potash glass was easier to engrave than *cristallo*, glassmakers experimented with ways to make glass that was harder, clearer and more brilliant. Success was achieved in 1683, when Michael Müller (1639–1709) added chalk to the recipe and produced a material that was ideally suited to cutting and wheel-engraving. Following this discovery, court engravers produced large, thick-walled vessels with ornate and often deeply cut designs.

In the sixteenth century, glassmakers in central Europe adopted the Venetian techniques of decorating vessels with gilding and enamel. Between about 1550 and the late eighteenth century, Bohemian and German workshops produced drinking vessels in great numbers: beakers, pitchers, tankards and above all large cylindrical vessels known as *Humpen*. Intended for groups of drinkers to consume beer in prodigious quantities, *Humpen* frequently bore gilded and enamelled coats of arms, such as the *Reichsadler*, the double-headed eagle of the Holy Roman Empire, which appears with the crucified Christ and, on its wings, the fifty-six shields of the member states.

The *Passglas*, which has a similar cylindrical form, is divided by applied trails into a series of horizontal bands. The name is derived from the custom, at drinking parties, of passing the glass from hand to hand. Each participant drank from the glass until he reached the next horizontal marker; if he missed the mark, he had to continue to the next – and so on.

Schwarzlot was another type of enamel decoration which, unlike the vivid palette used for painting *Humpen*, was dark brown and was usually employed to produce monochrome ornament. It was introduced in Nuremburg by Johann Schaper (1621–70), a painter of stained glass and *Hausmaler* of ceramics and glass. A *Hausmaler* (the German word means 'house painter') was a decorator who worked at home, painting objects on commission from manufacturers).

In the course of the eighteenth century, artists in the Low Countries, many of whom were amateurs, decorated glasses with a novel technique of cold-working. Diamond-point engraving, or 'stippling', consisted of tapping the glass with a hand-held tool tipped with a diamond. Each tap produced a bruise

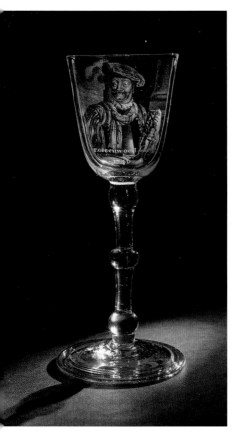

Below Frans Greenwood, a civil servant by profession, was a master of diamond-stipple engraving. Before Greenwood, diamond-point engraving was essentially linear. Between 1720 and 1722, he made the transition from line-engraving to rendering his designs with tiny dots. This portrait of an unknown man is signed by Greenwood and is dated 1746. H. 25 cm. Corning Museum of Glass, 50.2.10.

and the design depended on the density of the minute bruises; backgrounds and dark areas have few, while prominent and highlighted areas have a dense mass of tiny dots. The leading exponents of this technique were Frans Greenwood (1680–1763), who worked as a civil servant and decorated glass as a hobby, and David Wolff (1732–1787), who worked mostly at The Hague. Wolff is known to have signed and dated only nine glasses, but similarities of style have enabled experts to attribute some 200 unsigned pieces to him.

The British Isles, 1600–1800

At the beginning of the seventeenth century, the English parliament became seriously concerned about the destruction of forests by iron founders and glassmakers, and its possible impact on shipbuilding and the British navy. In 1610, a patent was awarded for making glass in a coal-fired furnace, but the venture failed. Three years later, Sir Edward Zouche (c.1556–1625) received a patent for a furnace of a different design. Later, the patent was extended to ban the use of wood as fuel and prohibit the importation of glass from Venice. The ban was reinforced in 1615 by a Royal Proclamation forbidding the use of wood by all glassmakers in England and Wales.

One of Zouche's associates, Sir Robert Mansell (c.1573–1652), bought out the other members of the company in 1614 and expanded the business, manufacturing glass vessels, mirrors and window glass. Employing Muranese workers, he produced Venetian-style glasses, probably including a popular form of wineglass with a hollow cigar-shaped stem.

During the Civil War (1642–51) and its aftermath, luxury goods were no longer in demand and the glass industry declined. It revived after the restoration of the monarchy in 1660. Glassmaking in general and the manufacture of window glass in particular received an additional boost when London was rebuilt after the Great Fire of 1666. A leading figure in this revival was George Villiers (1628–87), second Duke of Buckingham, who built glasshouses in and near London and had a virtual monopoly of mirror glass and impressive Venetian-style tableware. At the same time, large quantities of tableware were imported from Venice. Between 1667 and 1672, London glass-sellers imported no fewer than 28,000 pieces from the Venetian merchant Allesio Morelli.

In or just before the middle years of the seventeenth century, a new type of bottle had been developed in England. Made of dark green glass, it had a globular body, a tall neck and unusually thick walls. The thickness of the walls made the bottles strong, and they quickly became popular abroad as well as at home – so popular that, by 1695, English glassmakers were

Right This *Humpen* (literally 'mug' or 'drinking glass') celebrates the Treaty of Westphalia, which brought to an end the Thirty Years War, in 1648. God the Father looks down from Heaven and blesses the three rulers who signed the treaty: Emperor Ferdinand III, Louis XIV of France and Queen Christina of Sweden. Franconia, Germany, dated 1650. H. 26.4 cm. Corning Museum of Glass, 57.3.54.

Above Bernard Perrot (1619–1709) emigrated from Italy to France, where in 1668 he established a glass factory at Orléans. Among his discoveries was a method of casting large glass objects. He used this knowledge to cast portraits of King Louis XIV (r. 1643–1715), of which at least eight examples are known. Based on gold medals of the king made in the 1670s, the glass portraits are believed to date to the period 1675–85. H. (inc. frame) 38.7 cm. Corning Museum of Glass, 99.3.2.

Left The engraving on this covered goblet includes a royal crown above the monogram SCR. It refers to Sophie Charlotte, sister of George I of England and wife of Frederick I of Prussia. She was crowned queen (Regina: hence the final letter of the monogram) in 1701 and died in 1705. The goblet was made at Potsdam, near Berlin, Germany and engraved in 1701–1705. H. 31 cm. British Museum,1907,0726.1.

Below This wheel-engraved gold ruby beaker has silver-gilt mounts hallmarked in Augsburg, Germany and stamped 'TB', for Tobias Baur, who became a master goldsmith in 1685 and died in 1735. Gold ruby glass is transparent and coloured red by the addition of gold chloride. The method of making gold ruby glass was perfected by Johann Kunckel (1637–1703) in Potsdam, near Berlin, Germany shortly before 1679. This example was made in southern Germany, c.1700. H. 21.5 cm. British Museum, AF.3147, bequeathed by Sir Augustus Wollaston Franks.

producing nearly three million bottles annually. Many such bottles have applied seals which identify the taverns or private individuals who used them for beer and wine.

The desire to improve the quality of the glass used for fine tableware caused George Ravenscroft (1632–1689) to experiment with the addition of lead oxide to the raw materials. In 1673, he established the Savoy Glasshouse in London. His earliest experiments with lead were unsuccessful and the glass rapidly deteriorated on contact with moisture in the atmosphere. However, in 1676, he succeeded in making crystal-clear lead glass that remained in pristine condition. Ravenscroft marked his improved products with a seal decorated with a raven's head, which served as a guarantee that the glass would not deteriorate (see page 83).

Eighteenth-century English glassmakers produced superb vessels for drinking wine, ale and other beverages. At first, the shapes were simple and the decoration was confined to applied trails and moulded patterns that emphasized the clarity of the glass. Later, wine glasses with air-twist or colour-twist stems became popular, while the bowls might occasionally be decorated with wheel-engraved vignettes or mottoes, a few of which referred to the claims of the Stuart family, whose members occupied the throne until 1714, when the British crown passed to the house of Hanover. Plain glasses were much more common; but it is the decorated ones that have pride of place in public and private collections. The Jacobite ones, of which there are in fact a relatively small number – a tiny fraction of what was produced – have had a lot of attention from the salerooms and are rather valuable on the market.

Beginning in the 1760s, wineglasses and other shapes were not only sometimes engraved but also decorated with coloured enamels. The most prominent decorators were members of the Beilby family, notably William (1740–1819) and his sister Mary (1749–1797). Although the Beilbys painted glasses with floral motifs, landscapes and picturesque ruins, their most famous creations are large goblets decorated with royal coats of arms.

The nineteenth century
In central Europe, the period between the end of the Napoleonic Wars in 1814 and the revolutions that gripped Austria, France and other countries in 1848 was marked by the growth of a new middle class. As cities expanded and manufacturing became industrialized, a prosperous middle class emerged. The simple elegance of domestic architecture, furniture and decorative art favoured by the new bourgeoisie is known today as the Biedermeier style. The name was invented. In satirical verses,

Above Covered goblet with gadrooning on both the goblet and the cover, engraving and gilding. The bowl also has two medallions, one of gold ruby and the other of opaque turquoise glass, which are engraved and gilded with the monogram EP. This refers to Elizabeth Petrovna, daughter of Peter the Great, who seized the Russian throne in 1741 and ruled until her death in 1762. Potsdam, Germany, *c*.1750. H. 32.4 cm. British Museum, S.886, bequeathed by Felix Slade.

Adolf Kussmaul and Ludwig Eichrodt made fun of the middle class values represented by their fictional character Gottlieb Biedermeier (the German word Bieder means 'simple' or 'unpretentious').

Bohemian glassmakers flourished in the Biedermeier period and developed many new products. Georg Franz August Longueval (1781–1851) patented two opaque glasses, which he named '*hyalith*' (a combination of two Greek words, meaning 'glass' and 'stone'): black in 1817 and opaque red two years later. In 1828 Friedrich Egermann (1777–1864) patented 'lithyalin', a glass with marbled surfaces resembling semi-precious stones. At the same time, Anton Kothgasser (1769–1851) and others in Vienna, Bohemia and Dresden decorated vessels with exquisitely painted townscapes and landscapes, flowers and miniature portraits in transparent enamel.

At this time, the most accomplished Bohemian engraver was Dominik Biemann (1800–1857). Biemann led a somewhat itinerant existence, working in Prague and, in the season, at the spa of Franzenbad in western Bohemia, where he engraved portraits of visitors. His outstanding reputation is based on these portraits, which combine technical brilliance with great sensitivity.

The popularity of engraved and wheel-cut glass extended far beyond Bohemia. In France, for example, the leading manufacturer of fine tableware and display pieces, the Compagnie des Cristalleries de Baccarat, an old company renamed in 1823, produced fine cut and wheel-engraved glass, which won prizes at world fairs, such as the Exposition Universelle in Paris in 1867. In England and Ireland, cut glass was produced throughout the nineteenth century, although by 1900 its popularity had declined. The adoption, in 1807, of steam engines in power, meant that manufacturers using cutting wheels could produce large quantities of deeply-cut tableware, while engravers like the Bohemian William Fritsche (active in the 1870s) created vessels in the ornate 'rock crystal' style.

Chandeliers adorned with a multitude of prisms to reflect the candlelight became a prominent feature of interior design in the eighteenth century. On the Continent, the prisms were often made of rock crystal, while in England glass prisms became common in the 1820s. After windows, chandeliers were the largest objects made of glass in the eighteenth and early nineteenth centuries, although shortly after 1800 the Imperial Glassworks in St Petersburg created glass tables and other furniture for the palaces of the tsars.

The most successful English manufacturer of chandeliers was the Birmingham firm of F. & C. Osler. At the 1851 Great Exhibition in London, one of the first world's fairs, Oslers caused a sensation by exhibiting a giant glass fountain. Such was its success that the company opened showrooms in

Below In 1674, the English glassmaker George Ravenscroft applied for a patent to make colourless lead glass. His recipe was flawed and the glass crizzled. Ravenscroft revised the recipe and in 1776 he announced that the error had been corrected and his new glasses would be distinguished by a seal bearing a raven's head. On this goblet, it is at the bottom of the stem. H. 18.8 cm. Corning Museum, 50.2.2.

Right This ewer was made by Cristalleries de Baccarat and is a masterpiece of engraving. The narrow neck expands into a grotesque sea-monster's mask. The monster's scaly body and ivy wreaths in the spaces are wheel-engraved. France, c.1878. H. 31.9 cm. British Museum, 1991,0702.1.

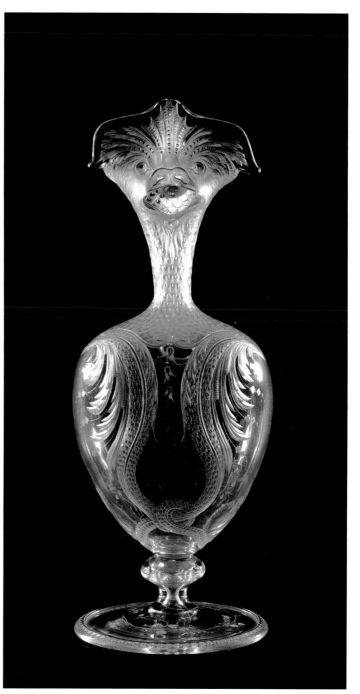

India, where they supplied royalty with chandeliers and cut-glass furniture, from occasional tables to chaises longues and thrones.

In the second half of the nineteenth century, throughout Europe much of the decorative glassware was made in imitation of earlier styles. In Bohemia, Austria and Germany, factories produced prunted beakers resembling green forest glass and enamelled *Humpen*, some of which are inscribed with fraudulent dates. Such dates were added for several reasons: to reproduce a broken original, to satisfy the taste for medieval and Renaissance décor, and to deceive gullible collectors. In Italy, the Venice and Murano Glass and Mosaic Company, inspired by Hellenistic and Roman originals, produced mosaic glass, some of which contain cane slices inscribed with a monogram to show that they are modern. Other Muranese glassmakers produced highly original canes containing portraits of leading personalities, including King Victor Emanuel III, Garibaldi and prime minister Cavour. The output of Salviati & C., another Murano factory, included copies of Renaissance glasses with gilded and enamelled ornament.

Other manufacturers turned to the Orient for inspiration. Some of Longueval's black hyalith glass was gilded with landscapes and other scenes recalling Japanese black lacquerware. In Vienna, J. & L. Lobmeyr marketed gilded and enamelled imitations of medieval lamps and other objects from the Islamic world, and in Paris, Philippe-Joseph Brocard's versions of Islamic glasses were so convincing that from time to time experts believed that they were the real thing.

Cameo glass, too, enjoyed a revival. The most famous Roman cameo glass, the Portland Vase (p. 33), had been brought to England in 1783, where it attracted widespread attention and became a source of inspiration for neo-classical design. The master potter Josiah Wedgwood (1730–95) produced jasperware replicas, the first of which appeared in 1789–90. The vase attracted other imitators, most notably the Englishman John Northwood (1836–1902), who completed the first glass replica of the vase in 1876. Subsequently, in the late nineteenth and early twentieth centuries, glassmakers in England and on the Continent made tens of thousands of cameo glasses for consumption both at home and abroad.

The history of English cameo glass was spectacular but short. Production was already under way in the 1870s but cameo glass was still a small business in 1885. Five years later, however, it was hugely popular and, thanks to the skills of George Woodall, his brother Thomas and a large team of decorators, the firm of Thomas Webb & Sons reaped a rich harvest as they strove to supply cameo glass to a seemingly insatiable market. The vogue

Right In the mid-19th century, as paper became cheaper and mail services improved, writing letters became a popular pastime. Glassmakers produced thousands of brilliantly coloured weights to hold down papers on writers' desks. The earliest datable paperweights were made in Italy in 1845. Soon afterwards, paperweights were manufactured in other parts of Europe and in the United States. This example, the famous 'Gingham' weight was made at the Compagnie des Cristalleries de Saint-Louis, France, c.1845–55. Diam. 8 cm. Corning Museum of Glass, 95.3.62.

Opposite George Woodall considered 'Moorish Bathers' to be his masterpiece. The plaque was carved by Woodall and his team at the factory of Thomas Webb & Sons in Amblecote, England. 'Moorish Bathers' depicts in minute detail a group of women in an exotic architectural setting. Begun about 1890 and completed in 1898, it is the largest and most ambitious of Woodall's many creations. Diam. 46.3 cm. Corning Museum of Glass, 92.2.10.

for cameo glass continued for a few years after 1900. Very soon afterwards, however, as fashion moved on, the handworking of cameo glass virtually ceased and a brilliant chapter in the history of English glassmaking ended.

Meanwhile, as the nineteenth century progressed, the glass industry became progressively more mechanized as the use of presses spread through Europe and America and machines were devised to produce repetitive acid-etched decoration that resembled engraving. At the same time, a reaction against mechanical production was gathering momentum under the leadership of John Ruskin (1819–1900), William Morris (1834–1904) and, in the field of glass, Emile Gallé (1846–1904), Louis Comfort Tiffany (1848–1933) and others (see pp. 102–119).

America

Opposite Bottles and windowpanes were the most common products of the glass factories of 18th-century America. This bottle bears a seal with the initials of Richard Wistar, son of the founder of Wistarburgh Glassworks at Wistarburgh, New Jersey, where it was made about 1745–55. H. 23.5 cm. Corning Museum of Glass, 86.4.196.

The first glass factories in the Americas were in Mexico (founded in 1535), Argentina (1592) and at Jamestown, Virginia (1608). All three were short-lived. The tiny factory at Jamestown was set up a year after the London Company of Virginia established a colony to provide timber, tobacco and other natural products for the English market. The factory was built and staffed by eight German and Polish glassmakers, with the intent of supplying the colony with such necessities as bottles and window glass. The venture was unsuccessful and the factory probably closed as soon as 1609. A subsequent attempt to revive the factory with Italian glassmakers failed and the last glass made at Jamestown before modern times was blown in 1624.

Elsewhere, the colonists also attempted to produce glass for local consumption: at Salem, Massachusetts (in 1641), Philadelphia (1682) and New Amsterdam (now New York, 1650s). None of these initiatives succeeded. Indeed, throughout the seventeenth century American colonists who could afford to do so relied on window panes, bottles and other vessels imported from England and the Low Countries. Between 1757 and 1773, George Washington imported 1,200 windowpanes, twenty-three dozen pieces of stemware and numerous other objects for use at Mount Vernon, his plantation in Virginia.

Wistar, Stiegel and Amelung

Glassmaking did not become firmly established in America until the second quarter of the eighteenth century. The first successful glassmaker was Caspar Wistar (1697–1752). An immigrant from Germany, Wistar settled in Philadelphia in 1717 and became first a maker of brass buttons and later an importer of German merchandise. In 1738, he decided to invest in glassmaking. He built a factory, Wistarburgh, in Salem County, New Jersey, and engaged four German glassmakers. According to his advertisements, Wistar's production consisted mainly of bottles and window glass for a growing population. His output was impressive: more than 15,000 bottles in

Left In addition to making bottles for everyday use, Henry William Stiegel, who established a glass factory at Manheim, Pennsylvania, in 1764, produced fine lead glass tableware. The only lead glass object that can be attributed with confidence to Stiegel is this wine glass engraved with the initials 'W & E OLD.' It was made to commemorate the wedding of Stiegel's daughter, Elizabeth, to William Old in 1773. H. 17.2 cm. Corning Museum of Glass, 87.4.55.

a typical year. Other products included tableware and scientific apparatus, such as Benjamin Franklin used in his experiments with electricity. Following the death of Caspar Wistar, the factory was managed by his son, Richard, until it closed about 1776. Made with similar materials (sand and potash) by immigrant workers, much of the Wistars' glassware resembled traditional Waldglas from Germany and Central Europe; indeed, expert opinion is often divided between those who believe an object to be imported and those who believe it was made at Wistarburgh.

Henry William Stiegel (1729–c.1780) was another German immigrant who succeeded as a glassmaker. Born in Cologne, Stiegel settled in Philadelphia in 1750. Employed by an ironmaster in nearby Lancaster County, he went on to become a partner in the company and in 1763 he opened a glass factory. The factory prospered and subsequently he opened The American Flint Glass Manufactory at Manheim. By 1769 he is reported to have opened a third glasshouse. Unlike Wistar, Stiegel produced fine English-style wine glasses, decanters and other tableware, sometimes with engraved decoration, in addition to glasses for everyday use. However, his ambition and expansive plans outran his pocket and in 1774, close to bankruptcy, Stiegel ceased to make glass.

The Revolutionary War (known in the United Kingdom as the American War of Independence) lasted from 1775 to 1783, disrupting trade and industry to the extent that no American glasshouse survived. Nevertheless, the Declaration of Independence (4th July 1776) freed local manufacturers and businessmen from British regulations, and local conditions favoured economic expansion. Glassmaking was subsequently revived by John

Above This covered tumbler bears the date 1788. It was made at the New Bremen Glass Manufactory of John Frederick Amelung. Inscribed 'Happy is he who is blessed with Virtuous Children,' the tumbler was presented by Amelung to his wife Carolina Lucia. The engraved scene depicts Tobias and the Angel. H. 21.4 cm. Corning Museum of Glass, 55.4.37.

Right Goblet made for Albert Gallatin in the New Geneva Glassworks at New Geneva, Pennsylvania, c.1798. The stem contains a silver medal awarded to Gallatin by the College of Geneva, Switzerland, in 1779, before he emigrated to the United States. From 1801–1814, he served as Secretary of the Treasury under President Jefferson. H. 23.5 cm. Corning Museum of Glass, 79.4.329.

Opposite 'Lily-pad' decoration was introduced to the United States by German glassworkers in the second quarter of the 19th century and it became popular in parts of the north-east. The lily-pad was made by collecting a second gather of molten glass around the end of the partly formed vessel and drawing it upwards in four or more projections with rounded ends. New York, c.1835–50. H. (bowl with cover) 27.2 cm. Corning Museum of Glass, 55.4.157.

Right When Benjamin Bakewell opened his factory at Pittsburgh in 1808, he resolved to make lead glass tableware. The upper part of this footed bowl, made between about 1815 and 1845 at the factory he founded, was blown in a mould to form the panels around the bottom, and engraved. H. 16.2 cm. Corning Museum of Glass, 94.4.9.

Frederick Amelung (1741–98). Amelung had gained experience of managing a glasshouse in his native Germany, where he assisted his brother, who leased the mirror factory owned by the Duke of Brunswick at Grünenplan, near Hanover. After securing financial support in Germany, he purchased equipment to build three furnaces. He hired glassworkers, and in 1784 sailed to America.

Amelung acquired a glass factory that had been built by some of Stiegel's workmen in Frederick County, Maryland, where forests provided fuel and potash, sand was available, and rivers and a road gave access to markets in Baltimore and beyond. Amelung's New Bremen Glass manufactory produced windowpanes and green and colourless tableware. The latter include beakers and goblets engraved with the names of politicians and businessmen. At first, Amelung prospered and by 1790 he operated four glass factories with 400 to 500 employees. His success, however, was short-lived and in 1795 Amelung, now bankrupt, closed the New Bremen factory. Ambition was his undoing. Like Stiegel, he made a large initial investment and his sales simply did not support the ongoing cost of maintaining four factories and several hundred employees.

The late eighteenth and early nineteenth centuries
Although Amelung was the most ambitious glassmaker in late eighteenth-century America, he was not alone. From New Hampshire to southern New

Left This decanter and stopper were made at the Boston & Sandwich Glass Works between about 1825 and 1835. The decanter, which bears the label 'RUM,' was blown in a full-size mould with three parts. Fragments of decanters with the same pattern of gothic arches and fern leaves have been found at the site of the factory. H. 27.5 cm. Corning Museum of Glass, 50.4.138.

Jersey, small factories supplied local markets with window glass and bottles, the standard products of early American glassmakers.

Meanwhile, the country was on the move. The newly independent government promised free land to anyone prepared to settle in the seemingly endless territory to the west of the original thirteen states. Settlers needed to construct houses and other buildings, and required utensils, and glassmakers were among the many manufacturers who hastened westwards to supply their needs. Pittsburgh was one of the gateways to the west, and it became a major source of provisions for pioneer settlers.

The first glass factories west of the Allegheny Mountains (that ran across West Virginia and Pennsylvania) were established by Albert Gallatin (1761–1849) and General James O'Hara (1752?–1819). Gallatin, who was born in Geneva, Switzerland, and is remembered as a long-serving secretary to the Treasury, opened a glasshouse in 1797 at New Geneva, on the Monongahela River, about fifty miles downstream of Pittsburgh. In the same year, O'Hara built a glass factory in Pittsburgh itself. O'Hara and his partner, Isaac Craig, advertised their windowpanes, bottles and other glassware at 25 percent less than the same items imported from the East Coast. Gallatin moved his factory across the river to Greensboro in 1804, where it continued to make window glass until 1847.

Window glass and bottles continued to be the mainstay of most American glasshouses in the early nineteenth century, although from time to time workers made glasses for the table, either for sale in local markets

Right Although thousands of 19th-century mould-blown flasks from America have survived, the actual moulds are exceedingly rare. The flask on the left was blown in the brass mould on the right, half of which survives. The subject is identified as Lafayette, a hero of the American Revolutionary War (1775–83), and the place of manufacture as 'COVETRY / C-T': evidently Conventry, Connecticut. The back of the flask has the initials 'S & S', the Coventry firm of Stebbins & Stebbins. H. (mould) 20.1 cm. Corning Museum of Glass, 60.4.87.

or for personal use. The items for personal use were made with glass that was left over at the end of the factory shift. These 'offhand' pieces, made with green or amber window or bottle glass, included pitchers, sugar bowls and other vessels and carried a distinctive lily-pad decoration: a ring of petal-like elements made by manipulating a second layer of glass gathered over the end of the vessel while it was still on the blowpipe. This popular motif, developed in Germany, was produced in America for much of the nineteenth century.

Although Amelung made colourless glasses with engraved ornament, the first major producer of cut glass in America was Benjamin Bakewell (1767–1844). Bakewell, who was born in England, opened a glass factory for fine lead or 'flint' glass tableware in his adopted home town, Pittsburgh, in 1808. Ten years later, at the request of President James Monroe, he supplied the first service of glass tableware for the White House, and in 1825 he presented two cut glass vases to the Marquis de Lafayette, a hero of the Revolutionary War (1775–83). Bakewell, Pears & Company (the name changed several times) thrived and continued to make glass until 1882.

Bakewell was the first, but not the only producer of lead glass in the early nineteenth century. During the War of 1812, when British ships prevented European goods from reaching America, Thomas Cains of the Boston Crown Glass Manufactory began to blow lead glass tableware. Not far away, in East Cambridge, Massachusetts, the New England Glass Company began to make a wide range of tableware and lighting devices in 1818. Beginning in 1826, Thomas Leighton, an experienced glassmaker from Scotland, managed the factory, which had about 140 employees – far more than any other American glasshouse. By this time, Deming Jarves, who formerly worked for the New England Glass Company, had opened the Boston & Sandwich Glass Company in Sandwich, Massachusetts. It was the third major glass factory within easy reach of the rapidly expanding port city of Boston.

Other cities, too, had suppliers of fine tableware: in 1824, Phineas and George Dummer established a glass factory in Jersey City, New Jersey, just across the Hudson River from New York, and in 1826 the Union Flint Glass Company started production at Kensington, then on the edge of Philadelphia.

The United States expanded rapidly in the first half of the nineteenth century. With the Louisiana Purchase of 1803, the government acquired the middle section of the country from France, settlers pushed farther and farther west, and California became the thirty-first state of the Union in 1850. Between 1800 and 1850, the country's population rose from five to twenty-three million.

The expansion of the United States and its population provided an enormous stimulus for industry and trade. Glassmaking flourished. The use of dip moulds or hinged two-piece moulds enabled glassmakers not only to form and decorate vessels in a single operation but also to produce large numbers of identical pieces. One of the most popular vessels made in two-piece moulds was an ovoid flask designed to contain whiskey and fit in the pocket. These 'pocket bottles' were decorated on both sides, sometimes with nationalistic symbols such as the American eagle, politicians or military heroes (see p. 93), and dozens of other motifs were available. Indeed, more than six hundred different designs are known. Pocket bottles were popular between about 1815 and 1865.

The introduction of pressed glass

A much greater step towards the mass production of glass occurred in the 1820s, when Benjamin Bakewell and others adopted a new technique: pressing. Hand-held presses had been used in eighteenth-century Europe to form small, solid objects, such as prisms for chandeliers. The new American presses (see p. 94), used in conjunction with moulds, reduced costs and at the same time increased productivity, making them the most effective innovation in glassmaking since the discovery of glass-blowing. A metal mould was placed in the press, molten glass was ladled into the mould and the operator pulled a lever, which drove a plunger into the glass, forcing it against the sides of the mould.

Mastering the glassblower's profession might take several years, but workers could be trained to operate presses in a matter of weeks, and a team of two operators could produce four times as many glasses as a team of three or four glassblowers. Decorated glass was no longer a luxury item and pressed objects became commonplace. The forms and ornament of the earliest pressed objects imitated cut glass. Later, a distinctive repertoire of overall 'lacy' patterns became popular. Few consumers realized that the intricate patterns had the practical purpose of concealing wrinkles caused when the molten glass came into contact with the much cooler surface of the mould.

Glass in the 'Gilded Age'

The Civil War (1861–65) had an impact on almost every aspect of life in America, and the glass industry was no exception. However, following the Reconstruction Era (1863–77), the economy revived in what the American author Mark Twain (1835–1910) called the 'Gilded Age'. Fortunes were made by investment in railways and the oil and steel industries, and the desire for luxury goods reached an unprecedented level.

The Centennial Exposition at Philadelphia in 1876 not only marked the hundredth anniversary of the Declaration of Independence but also celebrated the country's recovery. A local glasshouse, Gillinder & Company, exhibited a working glass factory, where they sold pressed glass souvenirs and displayed cut and engraved glass. Owning large, elaborate cut glass kerosene lamps, punch bowls and table services became a symbol of wealth and prestige, and the manufacture of cut glass expanded rapidly. The demand for cut glass, which survived until the First World War (1914–18), is well illustrated by the fortunes of Corning, New York. J. Hoare & Company established the first cutting shop at Corning in 1868 and eventually about twenty firms produced cut glass. Some were small, home-based cutting shops but others were large factories. At its peak around 1900, T.G. Hawkes & Company, which began operations in 1880, employed more than four hundred cutters and their assistants.

At the same time, brightly coloured and elaborately decorated ornamental glassware, usually known as 'Art Glass', became popular among middle- and upper-class Americans. The leading manufacturer of Art Glass was the Mt Washington Glass Company and its successor, the Pairpoint Corporation, in New Bedford, Massachusetts. Established in Boston in 1837, the factory was relocated to New Bedford in 1869. In 1880,

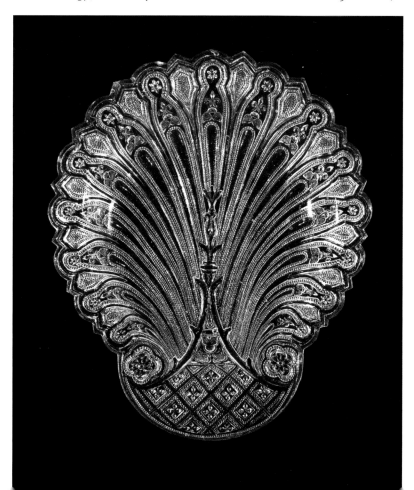

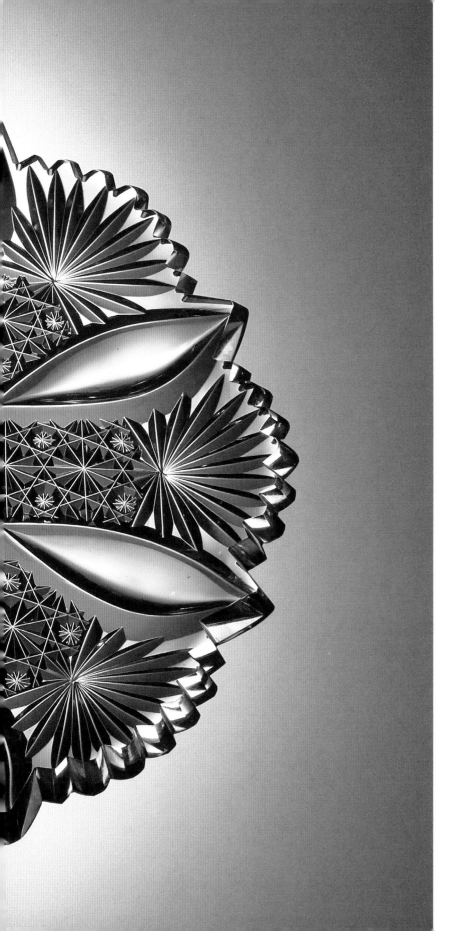

Plate cut in the 'Grecian' pattern by T. G. Hawkes & Company of Corning, New York. A report of 1902 described how cut glass was made in three stages: rough cutting with steel wheels, smoothing the cuts with stone wheels, and finally polishing with wheels made of poplar wood. Diam. 23.2 cm. Corning Museum of Glass, 2003.4.26.

the owners created the Pairpoint Manufacturing Company to make silver-plated wares, and the two businesses merged in the 1890s, becoming the Pairpoint Corporation in 1900. From 1869 to 1938, Mt Washington and Pairpoint made a great variety of decorative objects, tableware and lighting devices. One of America's most celebrated glass companies, around the turn of the twentieth century it had more than one thousand employees.

Between 1878 and 1897, Mt Washington produced an astonishing array of ornamental glassware, often with evocative names. Sicilian was introduced first, in 1878. Also known as Lava Glass, it supposedly contained lava from Mount Etna in Sicily. Sicilian was followed in 1885 by Burmese, with tones graduating from salmon pink at the top of the vessel to yellow at the bottom and with meticulous enamel decoration. The company also made Peach Blow, which shifts in shade from pink to bluish white, and Coraline, which has an overall pattern resembling branches of coral. Other products included Royal Flemish, Crown Milano and Napoli, names that were meant to catch the eye of the buyer, although none of the patterns had any connection with the Low Countries or Italy.

Art Glass was produced at a number of other factories, including the Boston & Sandwich Glass Company, the New England Glass Company and Hobbs, Brockunier & Company in Wheeling, West Virginia. It was Mt Washington, however, that advertised itself as the 'Headquarters for Art Glass in America'.

Artists discover glass

In March 1962, a groundbreaking workshop took place at The Toledo Museum of Art in Toledo, Ohio. Harvey Littleton (1922–), a professor of ceramics who had experimented with melting glass in a small furnace of his own design, joined forces with Dominick Labino (1910–87), director of research at a factory that made fibreglass. Together, they organized a week-long class intended to enable artists to construct a furnace, melt glass, and form it by blowing, casting, and flame-working. A second workshop was held three months later. The Toledo Workshops are widely regarded as the origin of the Studio Glass Movement, in which artists, mainly in the United States, began to work in their own studios instead of in factories. In the 1970s, the movement became international.

The forerunners
The Toledo Workshops did not happen in a vacuum. At the end of the nineteenth century, Emile Gallé (1846–1904) and Louis Comfort Tiffany (1848–1933) had explored the possibilities of glass as a medium for making art, in the factories they owned. Both were influenced by the Art Nouveau style of decoration which, in reaction against classicism and other historical revivals, favoured asymmetrical, sinuous lines inspired by nature. Meanwhile, in France, a small group of artists both designed and made glass objects, using the technique of *pâte de verre* (see Glossary), and, in the United States, Tiffany's rival Frederick Carder (1863–1963) designed a vast range of useful and decorative glassware in the Art Nouveau style.

Gallé was born and grew up in the Lorraine region of north-east France. He studied art and literature, and became an apprentice in his father's glass and ceramics factory at Nancy. In the 1880s, Gallé took over the management of the factory, bringing to the task a creative vision and an astute business sense. He became a leading designer in the Art Nouveau style and is admired today as much for his furniture designs as his glass. At the same time, Gallé was a campaigner for justice and a passionate

One of two glass and silver rose bowls from the 465-piece table service designed by Harry Powell and made at Whitefriars Glass Works for Count Lionel de Minerbi in 1906. The service was commissioned for Cà Rezzonico, the count's palazzo on the Grand Canal in Venice. The enamelled shields display his family's coat of arms. H. 27 cm. Corning Museum of Glass, 90.2.3.

Opposite 'La Libellule' (the Dragonfly Coupe), designed by Emile Gallé in 1903. Like many of Gallé's creations, the coupe combines imagination and originality with technical virtuosity. The object was blown, cased, embellished with hot-applied and inlaid decorative elements (including metal foil), cut, engraved and acid etched. H. 18.3 cm. Corning Museum of Glass, 80.3.59.

Below Vase designed by Frederick Carder about 1910. Carder named the iridescent effect 'Aurene,' combining the first three letters of aurum (Latin for 'gold') and the last three letters of schene (Middle English for 'sheen'). The applied decoration around the base recalls 19th-century American 'lily-pad' ornament (see page 91). H. 17.1 cm. Corning Museum of Glass, 75.4.113.

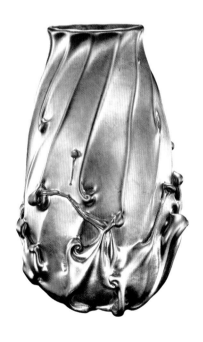

horticulturalist. He was also a writer with a profound admiration of the French Symbolist poets. Many of the highly original, complex and technically challenging glasses he designed embody his passion for nature and the philosophy of Symbolism. Gallé combined his skill as a designer and his appreciation of poetry in his inscribed 'vases parlantes' (speaking vessels). One of the most famous of these expresses Gallé's outrage at the false charge brought against Alfred Dreyfus, a Jewish officer in the French army, who was convicted of treason in 1894 and sent to Devil's Island, the notorious penal colony in French Guyana.

Tiffany, an American, inherited his father's business, Tiffany & Co., in 1920. Long before this, in 1879, he and several associates formed an interior decorating business and, when this was dissolved, Tiffany was sole proprietor of several companies that specialized in stained glass windows, mosaics and blown glass. As a young man, he travelled extensively in Europe and North Africa, absorbing historical European and Islamic motifs, which later became part of his eclectic design vocabulary. Tiffany's reputation as a glassmaker rests on his religious and secular windows, his leaded glass lamp shades and his blown objects, which included brightly iridescent 'Favrile,' opaque-pitted 'Cypriot' (inspired by ancient Roman glass) and textured 'Lava' glass.

In the field of glass vessels and ornaments, Tiffany's rival in America was Frederick Carder. Born in England, where he rose to be director of design at Stevens & Williams, a large glass works, Carder was persuaded to move to the United States in 1903. There he became head of design and a junior partner in the newly established Steuben Glass Factory in Corning, New York. The purpose of the new factory was to supply blanks to the local glass cutting establishment owned by Thomas G. Hawkes (the senior partner at Steuben) and to produce glass designed by Carder. Few glass designers have been more prolific than Carder, who completed one thousand designs by the end of 1905. Gold (and later blue) 'Aurene' glass had a brilliant iridescent finish similar to Tiffany's Favrile. In the 1920s, Carder continued to experiment with colours and techniques, and with ornament in the Art Deco style. In 1932, Steuben's new president decided to focus on colourless glass and to employ outside designers, who included John Gates, Sidney Waugh and Walter Dorwin Teague. Relieved of his position at Steuben, Carder concentrated on working alone, or with one assistant, to cast cire perdue (lost wax) sculptures, which included objects inspired by ancient Roman cage cups (pp. 37–9).

René Lalique (1860–1945), like Gallé and Tiffany, was another designer, who managed his own business. Born in France, Lalique studied graphic design in England before taking up residence in Paris, where he designed jewellery for Cartier and other well-known firms. In 1885, he acquired his own workshop and developed distinctive jewellery made from inexpensive metals and enamel, and decorated in the style of Art Nouveau. His display at the 1887 Exposition Universelle in Paris attracted the patronage of the actress Sarah Berhhardt (1844–1923) and cemented his reputation. In 1898, Lalique opened a glass workshop at Clairfontaine in northern France, where he designed perfume bottles for Coty and other leading manufacturers, and in 1910 he bought a glass factory at Combs-la-Ville in the south-east suburbs of Paris. He acquired another factory in 1919, at Wingen-sur-Moder, and here he produced large numbers of press-moulded vases, lighting devices, car mascots and other items, designed in the Art Deco style, which flourished in Western Europe in the 1920s and 1930s, and was distinguished by simple, streamlined shapes, non-representational motifs and often by the use of sumptuous materials.

While Gallé and Tiffany were creating highly original designs for the factories they controlled, a handful of French artists, working in their own studios, revived the supposedly ancient technique of *pâte de verre*, in which a plastic mixture of crushed glass and an organic binder was formed in a refractory mould (see Glossary) and fused in a kiln. The finished objects have a granular but sometimes wax-like surface reminiscent of marble. The revival of *pâte de verre* was led by Henry Cros (1840–1907), who about 1883 began to make plaques, fountains and freestanding sculptures. Other exponents, who in addition to small sculpture produced bowls and vases, included Georges Despret (1862–1952), Gabriel Argy-Rousseau (1885–1953), François-Emile Décorchemont (1880–1971) and Amalric Walter (1870–1959). Most of their early creations were unique objects, although later *pâte de verre* was sometimes used to produce limited editions.

Designers for industrial production
By 1860 John Ruskin (1819–1900), William Morris (1834–1904) and other British artists, critics and social reformers had become profoundly disturbed by the adverse effect of the Industrial Revolution on society and the arts. In 1861 Morris established a firm dedicated to reviving pre-industrial standards of design and craftsmanship. However, the extent to which essentially pre-industrial modes of production could ever provide for the needs of the rapidly increasing population was debatable and the Arts

Louis Comfort Tiffany designed this window in 1905 for the neo-gothic reception room of 'Rochroane,' a mansion at Irvington-on-the-Hudson, New York. A view of the river is framed by hollyhocks, blue and purple clematis and orange trumpet vines. The window is made entirely of coloured glass, sometimes with one piece on top of another; there is no paint or stain. H. 346.2 cm. Corning Museum of Glass, 76.4.22.

and Crafts Movement, as it came to be known, was criticized as 'the work of a few for the few.'

One approach to this paradox was to employ professional artists and designers to create items for production on a larger scale. Christopher Dresser (1834–1904) is often hailed as the one of the first industrial designers. Among his accomplishments in glass design were a silver-mounted set of tumblers and a decanter for Heath & Middleton (formerly Huth & Heath), which was made in 1882, and the 'Clutha' series of vessels for James Couper & Sons of Glasgow in the 1990s.

Ruskin, Morris and the Arts and Crafts Movement strongly influenced the philosophy of the Austrian architect and designer Josef Hoffmann (1870–1956). Hoffmann began his career in the studio of the influential architect Otto Wagner, and architecture occupied much of his working life. He also designed a wide variety of products, from furniture to glassware and wall paper. Between 1903 and 1932, many of his designs were produced by the *Wiener Werkstätte* (Viennese Workshop), a cooperative of painters, sculptors and decorative artists, which he founded in collaboration with Koloman Moser. Like Morris, the group believed that no object was so trivial that it could not be improved by fine design and execution. Hoffmann's glass designs included projects for two celebrated firms: Lötz Witwe and J. & L. Lobmeyr.

Glassmakers in Sweden adopted a different approach. In 1917 the Orrefors Glasbruk – hitherto a manufacturer of cheap domestic products – hired the painters Simon Gate (1883–1945) and Edvard Hald (1883–1980) to design high-quality glassware. Working with the master glassmaker Knut Bergqvist, Gate invented '*Graal*', a type of glass made by forming and annealing the object, cutting and engraving the surface, reheating it and finally casing it with a transparent outer layer. Later, in 1937, Bergqvist worked with the sculptor Edwin Öhsström to develop '*Ariel*', in which air bubbles are trapped within thick transparent glass.

Impressed by the success of Orrefors, in 1929 the Kosta Glasbruk hired Hagbard Ellis Bergh (1881–1954) as artistic director. Bergh's designs have the simple, almost severe forms and elegant cutting that came to typify much Scandinavian glassware of the mid- and later twentieth century. The most celebrated designer for Kosta (and other Swedish companies) was Viktor Emanuel (Vicke) Lindstrand (1904–1983), whose designs attracted attention at the Stockholm World's Fair in 1930, as did his monumental glass fountain at the New York World's Fair in 1939. Lindstrand's most famous design for an engraved glass vessel is 'Shark Killer', which Kosta first produced in 1937.

Sweden was not the only Scandinavian country to acquire a reputation
for finely designed glassware. In Finland, the Nuuajärvi Glassworks led the
way in 1905 by holding a competition for new designs for their domestic
glass, while in the 1920s and 1930s the Riihmäki factory produced designs
by Arttu Brummer (1891–1951). In addition to furniture, the architect and
city planner Alvar Aalto (1898–1976) designed glasses, most notably the
'Savoy' Vases (1936), which were made at the Karhula factory. After World
War II (post 1945), Tapio Wirkkala (1915–85), Kaj Franck (1911–89) and
Timo Sarpaneva (1926–2006) received international recognition for their
glass designs for Iittala and other Finnish glassmakers.

In Denmark, the Fyns Glasværker at Odense was the first manufacturer
to hire a designer, the painter Hans Andersen Brendekilde (1857–1942),
who designed Art Nouveau lamps, vases and other items in 1901–1904.
In 1924, the Holmegaards Glasværker entered into an agreement with
the Royal Porcelain Factory in Copenhagen to produce wine glasses to
accompany porcelain dinner services. Oluf Jensen (1871–1934) designed
the first set of glasses. Later designs were created by Orla Juul Nielsen
(1899–1928) and Jacob Bang (1899–1965). In 1942, Bang was succeeded by

Per Lütken (1916–1998), who produced more than three thousand designs for Holmegaard, including such iconic pieces as the 'Ideelle', 'Skipsglas' and 'Charlotte Amalie' sets of drinking glasses and 'Selandia', a tear-shaped dish.

Paolo Venini (1895–1959) and Giacomo Cappellin (1881–1968) were the leading figures in the developing modern glass design in Italy. Venini, who lived in Milan, set out to become a lawyer but quickly abandoned the idea. Cappellin, a Venetian, was an antique dealer with a gallery in Milan. In 1921, they joined forces and founded a glass factory in Murano, VSM Cappellin Venini & C. The artistic director was Vittorio Zecchin (1878–1947), a painter who drew inspiration from glasses depicted in the paintings of Veronese (1528–88) and Titian (1488/1490– 1576), but created the first modern designs produced in Murano. The clean lines of Zecchin's designs were much admired at the Paris Exposition of 1925.

That same year, however, the partnership was dissolved. Venini opened a new factory, Vetri Soffiati Muranesi Venini & C, while Cappellin opened a rival firm, Maestri Vetrai Muranesi Cappellin & C. Both factories had outstanding artistic directors. Venini employed Napoleone Martinuzzi

(1892–1977), many of whose richly coloured designs were variations on ancient forms. Martinuzzi also developed 'Pulegoso', a distinctive bubbly glass made by adding bicarbonate of soda or petrol, that was said to resemble the weathered appearance of ancient glass. At first, Cappellin employed Zecchin as his designer, but soon replaced him with a young architect, Carlo Scarpa (1906–1978), who quickly established his reputation as a designer, and was featured prominently in the influential magazine *Domus*, which Gio Ponti (1891–1979) founded in 1928.

In 1932, financial problems compelled Cappellin to close his factory. Venini, on the other hand, went from strength to strength. When Cappellin ceased production, Venini hired Scarpa, who remained with him until his retirement in 1947. During this period, the names of Venini and Scarpa were almost synonymous with the best of twentieth-century glass design in Murano and their large and varied output included '*Battuto*' (Beaten) vessels with a cold-worked, multifaceted surface resembling beaten metalwork, and the famous '*Fazzoletto*' (Handkerchief) vases. Other designers for Venini included Ponti, Tommaso Buzzi (1900–81) and Fulvio Bianconi (1915–76), who after World War II created the brightly coloured vessels known as 'Pezzati' (Patches).

The history of glassmaking in what is now the Czech Republic and in adjoining regions during the early twentieth century mirrored developments in Scandinavia and other European countries. The Republic of Czechoslovakia came into being in 1918, following the end of World War I and the dissolution of the Austro-Hungarian Empire. It occupied the most industrial part of the former empire and, between the two World Wars, it became one of the most prosperous countries in Europe. Among the educational initiatives of the new country was the creation of the Specialized School for Glassmaking at Zelezny Brod. After an uncertain beginning, the school took possession of a new building and began to flourish.

In 1921, one of the instructors at Zelezny Brod, Jaroslav Brychta (1895–1971), began to design whimsical flameworked figurines similar to figurines made at the Bimini Werkstätte in Vienna. He exhibited figurines at the 1925 Paris Exposition *Internationale des Arts Décoratifs et Industriels Moderne* (the term 'Art Deco' is derived from the name of this exhibition) and at the Brussels and Paris world's fairs of 1935 and 1937.

The spare functionalism taught at the Bauhaus at Dessau (the school in Germany that combined crafts and the fine arts, and was famous for its approach to design) by Walter Gropius (1883–1969) and his followers in and after 1919 strongly influenced Czechoslovakian glass designers.

'Anthem of Joy in Glass' was designed by the Czechoslovakian artist Veřa Lišková in 1977. The sculpture was constructed by flame working, in the course of which individual tubes were softened, stretched and fused. H. 99.5 cm. Corning Museum of Glass, 79.3.14.

Prominent among them was Ludvika Smrčková (1903–91), who designed useful and decorative objects for the Rückl glassworks at Nižbor. Other leading designers in this period included Josef Drahoňovský (1877–1938) and Jaroslav Horejc (1886–1983). Drahoňovský, a professor at the Prague School of Industrial Art, was a sculptor and gem-cutter, who designed and with his students engraved colourless vessels with classically inspired figures. Horejc's designs were intended for several media: metal, ceramics and glass. Some of his best-known glass designs were produced for the Viennese firm of J. & L. Lobmeyr in the early 1920s.

Artists in glass
A small number of early to mid-twentieth century artists worked with glass as their preferred medium. Two of these were a Frenchman, Maurice Marinot (1882–1960), and a Catalan, Jean Sala (1895–1976). Marinot began his artistic career as a painter and his initial interest in glass was as a vehicle for painting with enamel. Soon fascinated with glass as a plastic, Marinot persuaded friends to let him blow glass in the factory they owned at Bar-sur-Seine, France. Working alone at night, he produced massive sculptural vessels characterized by swirls of bubbles or colour, and sometimes with enamelled or acid-etched surfaces. Sala, who built his own furnace, also worked alone. He produced animals and small vessels, using either glass or *pâte de verre*.

Glass 1959
In 1959, the founding director of The Corning Museum of Glass, Thomas S. Buechner (1926–2010) organized Glass 59, an exhibition of contemporary glass, which was shown at Corning and five other museums in the United States. Glassmakers worldwide were invited to submit 'decorative and table glass made since 1955' to a jury of five, including designers George Nakashima and Gio Ponti, who chose the creations of 173 factories from twenty-three countries in North and South America, Europe and Japan. It was the world's largest-ever and most comprehensive exhibition of designs in glass.

The Toledo Workshops
In the same year, Harvey Littleton addressed the conference of American Craftsmen's Council at Lake George, New York, and proclaimed: 'Glass should be a medium for the individual artist'. At the Council's next conference in Seattle, Washington, Littleton and others discussed the possibilities of glass as a craft medium.

In 'Frosted Radio Light', American artist Paul Seide produced a rainbow-like effect by enclosing neon and other gasses in glass tubes. Neon was discovered in 1898 and by the 1920s neon lights were becoming a feature of the urban landscape. When an electrical current passes through neon, it produces orange or red. Other gases make different colours. In Paul Seide's piece, a transmitted radio field activates neon and mercury vapour. New York, United States, 1986. H. 48.4 cm. Corning Museum of Glass, 87.4.41.

Two direct outcomes of the meeting in Seattle were the 1962 workshops at The Toledo Museum of Art, where Littleton experimented with melting glass in a small furnace and Labino introduced glass that melts at a relatively low temperature. This combination of furnace and glass enabled artists to work with molten glass in their own studios rather than relying on access to hot shops in factories.

In 1963 Littleton began to teach glass-blowing at the University of Wisconsin, Madison. It was the first glassworking class in the curriculum of an American university. The next year, he held a four-week seminar. Several participants, including Marvin Lipofsky (b. 1938), went on to establish glassmaking programmes at other American universities. Meanwhile, Labino built a furnace and demonstrated glass-blowing at the World Congress of Craftsmen at Columbia University in New York. Erwin Eisch (b. 1927) from Germany, Sybren Valkema (1916–96) from the Netherlands and Harvey Littleton also took part in Labino's programme. Valkema, a teacher and co-director of the Gerrit Rietveld Academy in Amsterdam, went on to build the first small furnace for artists in Europe in 1965 and create the first hot-glass teaching programme, in 1969. Eisch, who worked in the family glass factory at Frauenau, also returned from the congress and built a small furnace. Working in the factory basement, he melted his own raw

'The Glass Wall' was designed by Brian Clarke in 1998 in Munich, Germany, as a tribute to his friend and collaborator, the photographer and musician Linda McCartney. It consists of seven panels, each with thirty-five panes. The recurrent *fleur-de-lis* is a reminder that lilies were Linda McCartney's favourite flowers. L. 22.4 m. Corning Museum of Glass, 99.2.4.

materials and developed a vision for glass as a sculptural medium.

Valkema and Eisch were not alone. In 1968, Asa Brant established the first small glassmaking furnace in Sweden. In the following year, Sam Herman established The Glasshouse in London and, five years later, he was instrumental in setting up a glassmaking facility at the Jam Factory Workshop in Adelaide, Australia.

At the Montreal Expo in 1967, glass sculptures in the Czechoslovakian pavilion astonished American glass artists. During the Cold War, the innovative work of the husband and wife team of Stanislav Libenský (1921–2002) and Jaroslava Brychtová (b. 1924), of Pavel Hlava (b. 1924), František Vísner (1936–2011) and others was virtually unknown in the West and their discovery had a profound impact. The impressionistic engraved portraits of Jiří Harcuba (b. 1928) had a similar startling effect and, beginning in 1983, he has taught the art of engraving to generations of students in Europe and the United States.

The American movement becomes international
During the 1970s, the Studio Glass Movement became international. Glass schools proliferated and galleries such as Habatat in Dearborn, Michigan and Heller Gallery in New York began to show and sell glass artists' work.

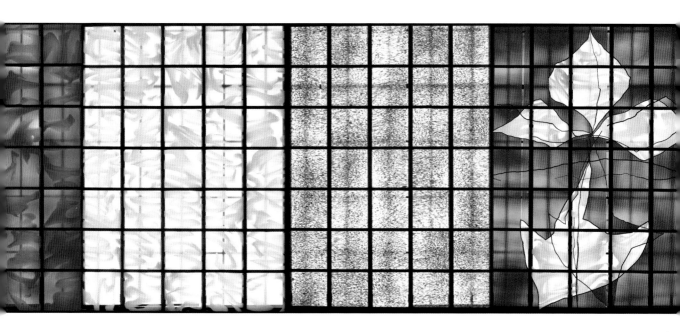

Exhibitions and publications increased. The Glass Art Society was founded in 1971. Also in 1971, the Pilchuck Glass School in Stanwood, Washington, was founded by Dale Chihuly and patrons Anne Gould Hauberg and John H. Hauberg; the school now hosts more than five hundred students every summer. In 1977, Buechner founded Contemporary Glass (renamed New Glass Review in 1980), an annual juried competition to select and publish one hundred works of art and design created anywhere in the world in the previous twelve months.

Twenty years after *Glass 1959*, The Corning Museum presented *New Glass: A Worldwide Survey*. The contrast between the two exhibitions and catalogues is startling. *New Glass* contained 196 works from twenty-eight countries and, in addition to being seen at American venues, the exhibition travelled to the United Kingdom, France and Japan. In *Glass 1959*, designers and factories submitted the majority of works; in *New Glass*, pieces made in the studio far outnumbered those produced on the factory floor. 'Glass', Buechner declared, 'has become a medium of the fine arts'.

As the numbers of artists, schools, commercial galleries and publications devoted to glass increase, the variety of techniques employed in the artists' studios is expanding. While glass-blowing flourishes in the hands of such masters as Lino Tagliapietra (b. 1934), Chihuly and William Morris (b. 1957), other techniques also attracted attention. Klaus Moje (b. 1936), Colin Reid (b. 1953) and Dan Clayman (b. 1957) are among the artists who form their work by slumping or casting glass in kilns. Bertil Vallien (b. 1938) and Howard Ben Tré (b. 1949) cast their sculptures in sand. Flame-working (the technique of softening glass rods and tubes in a concentrated flame in order to shape them and create composite objects) continues to gain in popularity, and the work of artists like Paul Stankard (b. 1943) and Gianni Toso (b. 1942) are avidly sought by collectors. *Pâte de verre* enjoyed a revival in the hands of Doug Anderson (b. 1952), whose 'Finders Creepers' was the first of the Corning Museum's annual Rakow Commissions, in 1986, and one of the largest and most complex examples of *pâte de verre*. Peter Aldridge (b. 1947) and Karen LaMonte (b. 1967) are among artists producing large-scale glass sculpture. At the other end of the scale, the number of beadmakers – they include Kristina Logan (b. 1964) – is legion, while Jacqueline Lillie (b. 1941) and Donald Friedlich (b. 1954) make delicate glass jewellery.

In the half-century since the Toledo Workshops, the number of artists working in glass has grown from a trickle to a flood. Glass is indeed a medium for the fine arts and artists on every continent are exploiting its unique properties. The work of such masters as Tagliapietra and Chihuly has taken its place in the mainstream of contemporary art and there have never been as many exhibitions, publications and collections of glass art as exist today.

Artists and other media

Several contemporary artists, who began work in other media, have experimented with glass. They include the sculptor Christopher Wilmarth (1943–87), the painter Robert Rauschenberg (1925–2008) and the sculptor and installation artist Donald Lipski (b. 1947).

Wilmarth was deeply influenced by the poetry of the nineteenth-century French Symbolist Stéphane Mallarmé. He established his reputation primarily as a sculptor, although he was also admired for his drawings and etchings. In his sculpture, he often combined glass with bronze or iron.

Rauschenberg, one of the first American Pop artists, achieved international acclaim in the 1950s. He enjoyed a long and prolific career, which included the creation of paintings, collages and installations. In 2005, he supervised the casting of a small series of colourless glass casts of car tyres, which represented a dirty industrial product as an object for contemplation.

Lipski works with mixed media, sometimes including in his work plants, such as carrots or aloes, floating in preservative solutions contained in repurposed glass containers manufactured for scientific or industrial use. The fluids preserve the plants from immediate decay, but they fade over time and transfer some of their colour to the liquid that surrounds them. The contrast between the tough containers and the vulnerable plants invites us to reflect on the fragility of the ecosystem that keeps us alive.

The future

The speed of change today makes forecasting a risky business. This is as true of technological change as changes in fashion or politics, and between the moment this book is written and the moment it appears in print, it is almost certain that new generations of glass and products that incorporate glass will appear.

It was not always so. The past really was a different country, where most changes came slowly. To the best of our knowledge, for more than two thousand years no-one realized that glass could be shaped by inflating a molten mass on a blowpipe, after which, for almost two thousand years, no-one devised a machine to replace glass-blowing by forming molten glass in a mechanical press.

But in the second half of the twentieth century, changes in the composition, manufacture and use of glass came in rapid succession. Today, to give just three examples, ultra-low-expansion fused silica mirrors are routinely employed in ground-based and space-borne telescopes; optical fibre has caused a revolution in communications; and defect-free glass with special properties is being perfected for liquid crystal displays. As scientists make increasing use of nanotechnology (the manipulation of matter on a molecular scale) to improve existing types of glass and devise new ones, the pace of change is likely to become even faster.

The versatility of glass

Developments in the appreciation of glass as a medium for creating art have been equally profound. In 1962, the Toledo Workshops (pp. 103 and 115) attracted just a handful of participants. Forty years later, the Glass Art Society has 1,840 members in forty-seven countries (they include artists, critics, collectors and dealers). In 1980, the first edition of *New Glass Review*, which chronicles the latest developments in glass art and design, featured artists from twelve countries, only one of which (Japan) was outside North America and Europe. The thirty-second, 2011 edition includes artists from twenty-four countries, six of which are outside those two core areas. The number of commercial galleries that sell glass art, and the number of museums and individuals who collect it, has grown exponentially. Clearly, glass has become a mainstream medium for making art, and year by year more artists explore new ways of using its unique properties.

Pliny the Elder summed up the uniqueness of glass: *neque est alia nunc sequacior materia . . . aut accommodatior* ('today no other material is more pliable . . . or adaptable than glass'). Pliny's words are as true today as they were more than nineteen centuries ago, and I expect they will be equally true in a hundred years' time.

'The Ionic Structure of Glass' is a composite panel created by one of the pioneers of Studio Glass, Dominick Labino (1910–1987), in 1979. Labino formulated his own batch (the mixture of raw materials) and researched new colours. Making good glass, he wrote 'requires years of study and experience ... but the exciting results ... are well worth the effort.' In this piece, he explored the effects of chemical reactions when layers of different glasses fused. Diam. 151.8 cm. Corning Museum of Glass, 80.4.30.

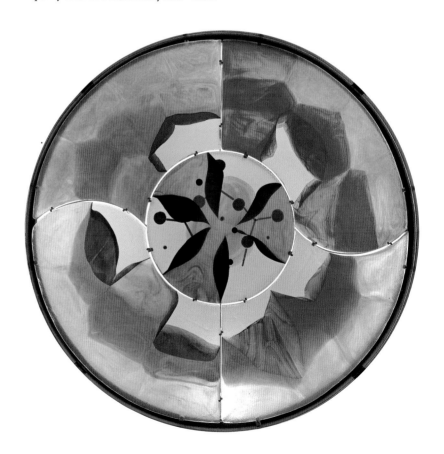

Glossary

This is a selective list of terms found in the text, which are not in daily use. Words that appear in **bold** in the definitions have their own entries elsewhere in the glossary.

Annealing The process of slowly cooling a completed object in an auxiliary part of the glass furnace, or in a separate furnace. This is an integral part of glassmaking because if a hot glass object is allowed to cool too quickly, it will be highly strained by the time it reaches room temperature; indeed, it may break, either as it cools or at a later date. Highly strained glasses break easily if subjected to mechanical or thermal shock.

Blank In glassworking, any cooled object that requires further forming or decoration to be finished.

Blown glass Glassware formed by inflating a mass of molten glass on the end of a blowpipe. The glassblower produces the desired form by swinging the molten glass, rolling it on a smooth surface, manipulating it with tools, or shaping (and sometimes decorating) it in a mould.

Cage cup A vessel decorated by undercutting, so that the surface stands free of the body of the glass, to which it is attached by struts.

Cameo An object, generally small, carved in relief from stone or some other material that has bands of contrasting colours, so that different parts of the decorated surface display different colours.

Cameo glass Glass of one colour covered with one or more layer(s) of contrasting colour(s). The outer layer(s) is/are carved, cut, engraved or (in modern times) acid-etched to produce a design that stands out from the background. Roman cameo glass **blanks** were either **cast** or **blown** using the dip-overlay technique, whereby an elongated bubble of glass was partially dipped into a crucible (fire-resistant container) of white glass, before the two were blown together. After cooling the white layer was cut away to form the design.

Cast glass The generic name for a variety of techniques used to shape molten glass by placing it in or on a form or mould.

Cold-working The collective term for mechanical techniques (such as cutting, grinding and copper-wheel engraving) used to alter or decorate glass after it has been annealed.

Dip-mould *See* **mould-blown glass**

Egyptianising Formed or decorated in a style that resembles Egyptian art or design.

Enamelled decoration In glassmaking, enamel is a vitreous substance made of finely powdered glass coloured with an oxide and suspended in an oily medium for ease of application with a brush. The enamel is fused to the surface of the object by firing it in the mouth of the furnace or in a kiln. When the enamel is fired, the medium burns away.

Fusing (1) The process of founding or melting the raw materials; (2) heating pieces of glass in a kiln or furnace until they bond; (3) heating enamelled glasses until the enamel bonds with the surface of the object.

Gather A mass of molten glass collected, usually, on the end of a blowpipe.

Hydrofluoric acid A highly corrosive acid that attacks glass and other silicates. Pure hydrofluoric acid dissolves glass leaving an etched or acid-polished surface.

Lathe-turning The technique of mounting a **blank** on a lathe and (in antiquity) turning it with the aid of a bow or a wheel with a handle, often while a tool fed with an abrasive is held against the surface in order to cut, grind or polish it.

Mould-blown glass This is the result of inflating the bubble of hot glass inside a decorated mould. Traditionally, moulds are of two kinds. 'Dip' or 'optic' moulds, shaped like beakers, are used to impart a pattern, after which the bubble of glass is withdrawn and blown to the desired shape and size. 'Full-size' moulds, with two or more hinged parts, are used to shape and decorate the object at the same time.

Obsidian A volcanic mineral, usually black, that was the first form of natural glass used by humans to make tools and weapons.

Opaque Impervious to the rays of visible light. See also **translucent** and **transparent.**

Parison A **gather**, on the end of a blowpipe, that is already partly inflated.

Pâte de verre (French, 'glass paste') A material produced by grinding glass into a fine powder, adding a binder to create a paste, and adding a fluxing medium to facilitate melting. The paste is brushed or tamped into a mould, dried, and fused by firing. After annealing, the object is removed from the mould and finished.

Potash Potassium carbonate. It is an alternative to soda as a source of alkali in the manufacture of glass.

Prunt A blob of glass applied to a glass object primarily as decoration, but also to afford a firm grip in the absence of a handle.

Silica Silicon dioxide, the main ingredient of glass. Sand is the source of almost all the silica used in glassmaking.

Slumping The process of reheating a blank until it becomes soft and gradually flows under its own weight over or into a former mould and eventually assumes the shape of the mould. Also known as sagging.

Tazza In descriptions of glass, a shallow cup or bowl with a stem and a foot.

Translucent An adjective describing a substance that transmits light but through which objects cannot be seen. Although translucent and **transparent** are sometimes used as synonyms, they have different meanings. *See also* **opaque.**

Transparent An adjective describing a substance through which objects can be seen. *See also* **opaque** and **translucent.**

Weathering Changes on the surface of an object caused by chemical reaction with the environment. Weathering of glass usually involves the leaching of alkali from the glass by water, leaving thin layers of siliceous weathering products.

Further reading

General
Reino Liefkes and others, *Glass*, Victoria and Albert Museum, London, 1997.
Jutta Annette Page and others, *The Art of Glass*, Toledo Museum of Art, Toledo, Ohio, 2006.
Hugh Tait and others, *Five Thousand Years of Glass*, revised edn, British Museum Press, London and University of Pennsylvania Press, Philadelphia, 2012.
David Whitehouse, *Glass: A Pocket Dictionary of Terms Commonly Used to Describe Glass and Glassmaking*, revised edn, The Corning Museum of Glass, Corning, New York, 2006.

Introduction: glass and glassmaking
Charles Bray, *Ceramic and Glass: A Basic Technology*, Society of Glass Technology, Sheffield, 2000.
Ed Burke, *Glass-blowing: A Technical Manual*, The Crowood Press Ltd, Ramsbury, 2005.
Keith Cummings, *A History of Glassforming*, A & C Black, London, 2002.
Henry Halem, *Glass Notes: A Reference for the Glass Artist*, fourth edn, Franklin Mills Press, Kent, Ohio, 2006.

Glass before glass-blowing
David Frederick Grose, *The Toledo Museum of Art: Early Ancient Glass*, Hudson Hills Press, New York, 1989.
E. Marianne Stern and Birgit Schlick-Nolte, *Early Glass of the Ancient World, 1600 BC AD 50: Ernesto Wolf Collection*, Verlag Gert Hatje, Ostfildern, 1994.

The glass of ancient Rome
Donald B. Harden, Hansgerd Hellenkemper, Kenneth Painter and David Whitehouse, *Glass of the Caesars*, Olivetti, Milan, 1987.
E. Marianne Stern, *The Toledo Museum of Art. Roman Mould-Blown Glass: The First Through Sixth Centuries*, 'L'Erma' di Bretschneider, Rome, 1995.
E. Marianne Stern, *Roman, Byzantine, and Early Medieval Glass, 10 BCE–700 CE: Ernesto Wolf Collection*, Hatje Cantz Publishers, Ostfildern-Ruit, 2001.

From Rome to the Renaissance
Jennifer Price, ed., *Glass in Britain and Ireland, AD 350–1100*, British Museum Occasional Publication Number 127, The British Museum, London, 2000.

Rachel Tyson, *Medieval Glass Vessels Found in England, c. AD 1200–1500*, Council for British Archaeology, York, 2000.

David Whitehouse and others, *Medieval Glass for Popes, Princes, and Peasants*, The Corning Museum of Glass, Corning, New York, 2010.

The Islamic world and Eastern Asia

Robert H. Brill and John H. Martin, eds., *Scientific Research in Early Chinese Glass*, The Corning Museum of Glass, Corning, New York, 1991.

Claudia Brown and Donald Rabiner, *Clear as Crystal, Red as Flame: Later Chinese Glass*, China House Gallery, New York, 1990.

Stefano Carboni, *Glass from Islamic Lands*, Thames and Hudson, New York, 2001.

Stefano Carboni and David Whitehouse, *Glass of the Sultans*, The Metropolitan Museum of Art, New York, 2001.

Renaissance and early modern Europe

Robert J. Charleston, *English Glass and the Glass Used in England, c.400–1940*, George Allen and Unwin, London, 1984.

Olga Drahotová, *European Glass*, London, Peerage Books, 1983.

Catherine Hess and Timothy Husband, *European Glass in the J. Paul Getty Museum*, J. Paul Getty Museum, Los Angeles, 1997.

Dedo von Kerssenbrock-Krosigk, *Glass of the Alchemists: Lead Crystal–Gold Ruby, 1650–1750*, The Corning Museum of Glass, Corning, New York, 2008.

Brigitte Klesse and Hans Mayr, *European Glass from 1500–1800: The Ernesto Wolf Collection*, Kremayr & Scheriau, Vienna, 1987.

Dwight P. Lanmon, *The Golden Age of English Glass, 1650–1775*, Antique Collectors' Club, Woodbridge, Suffolk, 2011.

Jutta Annette Page and others, *Beyond Venice: Glass in Venetian Style, 1500–1750*, The Corning Museum of Glass, Corning, New York, 2004.

America

Arlene Palmer, *Glass in Early America*, Henry Francis du Pont Winterthur Museum, Winterthur, Delaware, 1993.

Kenneth M. Wilson, *The Toledo Museum of Art: American Glass*, Hudson Hills Press, New York, 1994.

Artists discover glass

Victor Arwas, *Glass: Art Nouveau to Art Deco*, Academy Editions, London 1987 and Harry N. Abrams, Inc., New York, 1987.

Susanne K. Frantz, *Contemporary Glass: A World Survey from The Corning Museum of Glass*, Harry N. Abrams, Inc., New York, 1989.

Martha Drexler Lynn, *American Studio Glass 1960–1990: An Interpretive Study*, Hudson Hills Press, Mancher, Vermont, 2004.

Tina Oldknow, *Voices of Contemporary Glass: The Heineman Collection*, The Corning Museum of Glass, Corning, New York, 2009.

Helmut Ricke and Eva Schmitt, *Italian Glass, Murano Milan, 1930–1970: The Collection of the Steinberg Foundation*, Prestel, Munich and New York, 1997.

William Warmus and Beth Hylen, *The Chronology and Bibliography of Studio Glass*, www.warmus.com.

Additional titles

Two major aspects of glassmaking, not covered in this book, are stained glass, which has a history that spans more than a thousand years, and modern industrial glass. The following titles provide introductions to these subjects:

Stained glass

Catherine Brisac, *A Thousand Years of Stained Glass*, Chartwell Books, Edison, New Jersey, 2000.

Madeline Caviness, *Stained Glass Windows*, Brepols, Turnhout, Belgium, 1996.

Painton Cowen, *English Stained Glass*, Thames & Hudson, London, 2008.

Patrick Reyntiens, *The Beauty of Stained Glass*, Herbert, London, 1990.

Industrial glass

Anon., *Innovations in Glass*, The Corning Museum of Glass, Corning, New York, 1999.

Heinz G. Pfaender, *Schott Guide to Glass*, Chapman & Hall, London, 1996.

Fay V. Tooley, *The Handbook of Glass Manufacture*, third edn, Ashlee Publishing Co. Inc., New York, 1984.

For additional Information, readers may consult two other publications of The Corning Museum of Glass. The *Journal of Glass Studies* is an annual publication containing articles on all aspects of glass and glassmaking before the mid-20th century. Volumes 1 (1959) to 46 (2004) include a 'Check List' of recent books and articles on glass. The checklist went online (at http://rakow.cmog.org) in 2003.

Beginning in 1980, the Museum also publishes *New Glass Review*, an annual survey of contemporary glass containing one hundred new works of art or design selected by a jury, and essays by the jurors.